CHECK
IT OUT !

CHECK IT OUT!

EDMUND J. PANKAU

CB

CONTEMPORARY
BOOKS

CHICAGO

Library of Congress Cataloging-in-Publication Data

Pankau, Edmund J.
    Check it out! / Edmund J. Pankau
       p.   cm.
    Includes bibliographical references.
    ISBN 0-8092-3945-0
    1. Public records—United States—States—Handbooks,
manuals, etc. 2. Biography—Research—Methodology—
Handbooks, manuals, etc. 3. Investigations—Handbooks,
manuals, etc. I. Title.
JK245.P82P36   1992
353.0071′4′0202—dc20

                                              91-39262
                                            CIP

Published by Contemporary Books, Inc.
180 North Michigan Avenue, Chicago, Illinois 60601
Manufactured in the United States of America
International Standard Book Number: 0-8092-3945-0

CONTENTS

ACKNOWLEDGMENTS

I would like to thank all of my clients whose true stories are the basis and reason for the publication of this book. Because they brought me their problems, I can, I hope, provide the answers to solve yours.

I would also like to thank several of my colleagues who have supported my ideas, however radical, and who share the ideals and goals of developing a true professional investigative industry. These people include:

Joseph Wells, chairman, National Association of Certified Fraud Examiners, Austin, Texas.

Ralph Thomas, director, National Association of Investigative Specialists, Austin, Texas.

Peter Ohlhausen, senior editor, American Society for Industrial Security, Arlington, Virginia.

Walter Johnson, chairman, Southwest Bank of Texas, Houston, Texas.

My most special thanks go to two people who helped make this all possible:

Royce Till, attorney, Fulbright & Jaworski, Houston—for giving me a chance to show him what I could do.

Lew Vail, who took my ideas and built them into the computer and has worked with me for almost eighteen years.

I sincerely thank all of these people. Their help, support, and advice have helped more than I can ever say.

CHECK IT OUT!

FOREWORD

If there is one man who stands out in the P.I. business, it's got to be Ed Pankau, founder and chairman of Houston-based Intertect, Inc.

Ed Pankau has been featured in *Time, USA Today*, and the *Wall Street Journal* and on ABC's "20/20" for his investigations of the nation's biggest financial frauds. He is also the spokesperson for investigators, regulators, and the American public, all of whom want to know the answer to *Where are the swindled savings?*

After leaving the government as a special agent for the prestigious IRS Organized Crime Division in 1972, Ed started a traditional one-man private investigation business, surveilling errant spouses, proving insurance frauds, and holding lawyers' hands in court. Through his investigations and his testimony at trials, he soon got a reputation as the man to hire for tough cases.

In 1978 his firm's business became focused in a new area as a result of the investigation of failed banks and savings and loan institutions. Because of his background in financial investigations, Pankau was hired by lawyers at the Federal Deposit Insurance Corporation (FDIC) to investigate five failed banks in Houston, Texas, and to help the government recover millions of dollars lost through phony borrowers and crooked bank officers who looted the institutions.

Through his investigation of these failed institutions,

Ed saw a pattern that would become apparent time after time in banks and S&Ls throughout the country. Pankau foresaw that the problems found in Texas banks would spread all over the country and that our nation's banks and S&Ls, from Texas to Massachusetts to California, were riddled with fraud, waste, and abuse.

Local reporters investigating the S&L scandal came to Pankau and used his information to show stories on national television about the problems in Texas banks. On programs like "The McNeil/Lehrer NewsHour" and "20/20," Pankau asserted that fraud existed in more than half of the failed banks and predicted that this situation would escalate into the biggest single problem our nation faced, a problem so big that it might cause a national depression.

To combat the growing losses in these financial institutions and to meet the investigative demands of government regulators, someone had to develop a new investigative technology, a Henry Ford system of searching public records, computer databases, and other esoteric information sources to develop a financial profile and history of the con artists who took our money. This system had to be teachable and capable of standardization so that a report generated in St. Louis could be integrated into a report done in Florida or Texas, then used by regulators and their attorneys to make a litigation decision on their subjects.

Through an analysis of the common threads in the hundreds of bank fraud cases Pankau investigated and his background experiences, both as an accountant and as investigator with the IRS Organized Crime Division, Ed Pankau developed a format for detecting undisclosed business interests and finding hidden assets. He then brought all of the various public records into his office, where they could be researched and analyzed quickly and efficiently.

In creating this investigative assembly line, Pankau revolutionized the private investigation business in a way that now affects everyone in the industry. Work that used to take days or weeks can now be done day or night, often in a matter of hours. The computer-literate investigator can solve cases at one-third the previous cost and thus be able to charge a more affordable fee while still making more profit than under the old manual methods.

Within a few years, investigators all over the country learned this technology through professional seminars led by Pankau for the Investigators Online Network, the American Society for Industrial Security, and the National Association of Certified Fraud Examiners. Many of those who heard and saw Pankau's seminars went home, bought a computer, and "plugged in" to databases all over the world: newspapers, public record sources, and financial databases that let them do research any time they wanted. The world would never be the same.

When the economic minister of Colombia embezzled $12 million and fled, Pankau tracked his daily movements by his hotel and restaurant charges found through a hidden American Express account.

Airline travel records helped Pankau track three international check kiters who skipped from Mexico to the United States. Before their plane landed in Dallas, Pankau and federal agents set up a reception committee that collected the thieves and returned 27 billion pesos.

With an Assumed Name Certificate filed in public records, Pankau brought down a millionaire bank executive who hid his undisclosed business interests in his wife's maiden name. Once Pankau had found her maiden name in marriage records and compared it against bank vendors, regulators charged the officer with fraud and sued for millions of dollars.

A long trail of lawsuits led to the downfall of a slick movie theater owner who moved from town to town ahead of his creditors but could not escape the computerized investigator, Ed Pankau. Pankau's exposure of Tony Rand's legal history and financial schemes made the front page of the *Wall Street Journal* and ended Rand's "movie career."

Today, much of Ed's time is spent giving seminars on money laundering, hidden asset location, and fraud detection to federal regulators, police detectives, private investigators, and people like you and me who want to learn the tricks of the trade. As a hobby, Ed writes a weekly column on fraud protection for a local newspaper and frequent articles for professional and trade publications.

Late at night you can still find him behind his desk, studying cases and directing his staff of investigators. He loves and believes in his work and truly feels that his efforts have made a difference in the war on white-collar crime.

Thus, I'm proud to introduce to you Ed's new book, *Check It Out!*. Within its pages, you will find some of the best techniques and insights from one of the most successful private investigators in the United States today. And now find out for yourself—check it out!

Ralph Thomas, Director
National Association of Investigative Specialists
Austin, Texas

INTRODUCTION

- You're planning to marry the love of your life.

- Monday you're going to hire an apparently gifted new employee.

- Your small company is about to add a new partner.

- You're going to be negotiating a tough lease with an out-of-town tenant.

- Your news editor has assigned you to investigate a local fraud.

- Your bank is evaluating a substantial business loan for a new company.

These life situations share a vital common ingredient. If any of these scenarios applies to you, then you need information and fast. This book will teach you how to obtain detailed information about another person or organization.

From my own years as an investigator, I know that this need for information applies to everyone. If people were wise, it *should* mean everyone.

Fortunately, to aid your own quest for these facts, there is at your disposal a treasure trove of public records that for the most part are easy to access and will provide or point you toward much of the background information you may be looking for. These public records are the same ones I use to initiate every major investigation my company ever conducts—from complex criminal frauds responsible for so many bank failures, including the largest check-kiting conspiracy in Mexican history, to locating just in time a sociopathic bigamist who was about to abduct and murder his latest spouse.

In this book, you'll find out which public records to search whenever you need to know the background of an individual or organization. You'll also learn techniques that will help you do that research more efficiently. You'll discover the extraordinary value of public records, and you'll know what signals should warn you to steer clear of a person or his or her proposal.

Let me reassure you that your desire to know, to really know, the truth about the people with whom you do business, or hire, or use as witnesses, or marry is not just nosiness or paranoia. Far from it. It's self-defense and just plain common sense.

Even though I am a professional investigator, I try hard never to become jaded when it comes to personal backgrounds. That's tough, though, because I'm exposed so often to the darker side of society and to some of its least attractive elements: cons, frauds, charlatans, cheats, thieves, dope dealers, addicts, sex offenders—even killers. These despicable characters can turn up in your life when you least expect them and sometimes even in places and circumstances where you would *never* expect them.

Unfortunately for you and other victims, the shrewdest of this lot, those most adept at their particular aberration, are also the most difficult for you to spot—especially if you're depending on your own instincts or on the carefully crafted information these cons are selling you. Hopefully, these characters will not show up in your life very often, but it takes only one to make your existence miserable, to cause you enormous hardship, to become your worst nightmare.

When I say that sooner or later everyone may need to obtain valid background information on someone else, I mean everyone: lawyers to lovers, bankers to businesspeople—literally anyone who ever gets involved with someone they don't know well.

And, yes, that includes journalists trying to track a story, develop leads or background on someone before an interview, or verify what a subject has admitted or revealed. It also includes lawyers trying to locate missing or elusive witnesses, lawsuit targets, or hidden assets. The list is virtually endless.

My firm, Intertect, Inc., is often called in by businesses to conduct background searches when our clients are hiring, merging, acquiring, or completing significant financial transactions. Unfortunately, all too often, by the time we are hired our clients are already deeply involved in the problems caused by unscrupulous characters.

If those victims had only taken the trouble to check the public records available to anyone, or if they'd hired Intertect (or someone like us) sooner instead of relying solely on the information provided by the person hustling them, they could have avoided a disastrous financial loss, personal stress, or public humiliation.

So use this book well. Study it. I sincerely believe that if you apply these techniques diligently, you can find out almost anything you need to know about anyone in your life and avoid being victimized by frauds or con artists. After reading the book, you might discover you don't have time to chase down leads on your own. But at least you'll be aware of how and where to find the information you need to protect yourself from the sharks. And you always have the option of hiring a professional investigator with a clearer idea of what you need and how successful he or she might be on your behalf.

Whatever you do, never ignore or put off the decision to look into the people who are about to become a big part of your life. Follow the advice in this book, and you too can avoid your worst nightmare. That's a *promise*.

1

GETTING PERSONAL

How can you, the average citizen, without a badge, gun, or subpoena, find the facts you need to make your critical personal and business decisions? By searching the many publicly available records.

PUBLIC RECORDS AND WHERE THEY ARE FOUND

Public records are information about people, businesses, or organizations available legally to anyone without subpoena, subterfuge, or midnight trash runs.

In truth, so much public information is available about people's pasts, identities, and activities that it is nearly impossible for a common fraud or con artist to pass a thorough background search without detection or at least without the appearance of certain warning signs that would indicate a need for further examination.

Generally, you will find public records in two main

locations: government agencies and the databases of private industry.

Government Agencies

Every level of government maintains a broad collection of records on individuals that identifies them and documents their individuality.

City government records often include utilities filings, traffic court records, building permits, and business and occupational licenses.

Every county keeps voter registrations, auto registrations, marriage and divorce records, deed transfers, property tax rolls, assumed business names, records of civil litigation, and criminal histories, to mention a few.

State records include incorporation records, assumed name information, notary registrations, driving records, professional and licensing registrations, and criminal arrest and conviction records.

The federal government maintains military records, Social Security information, bankruptcy filings, immigration records, passport information, all international commerce registrations, and a host of regulatory business documents.

Then, of course, there are the courts at all levels from local to federal, which also keep pertinent information on civil and criminal actions in their jurisdictions.

Private Industry Databases

There are myriad independent and private services that keep records as part of their businesses or for professional organizations.

2

Telephone books, crisscross directories, and computer on-line cross-references are quick and simple sources for checking current and past addresses and telephone numbers, and for locating neighbors who may have information about a subject who moved recently.

Professional organizations, associations, and registrars publish and distribute yearbooks of members, often including photographs, which can be quite valuable in zeroing in on your target. These publications list doctors, lawyers, nurses, real estate agents, pilots, insurance agents, and many others. You can find professional people in regional and national who's who directories categorized by occupation, name, and home address.

While these ideas are not all-inclusive, they give you some idea of how much is out there to help you check out anyone's background. Chances are you won't need to use all these sources for the checks you will do yourself, especially if your investigation is for a specific purpose, such as for credit, hiring, or dating reasons. But in most cases, this outline will give you an idea of the type of records you need, so stick to them. If you want to review the background of someone you're about to marry or go into business with, then your search may need to be more extensive.

As you will soon see, there is plenty that you, on your own, can do to run a thorough search on anyone for any reason.

A Note on Obtaining and Using Public Records

Many public records can be purchased from compiling organizations at minimal cost. Voter registrations are an example. Most counties in major metropolitan areas sell voter registration records on microfiche. However, what you get when you purchase the registrations is not the actual registration form, but indexes of the names and addresses, dates of birth, and often Social Security numbers. Often, you may need to go in person to the records office to examine a subject's actual documents to compare signatures or find other information. This might also be true for other public records at their actual repositories.

Later, I'll offer you tricks of the trade to use when you examine documents at the courthouse.

Did you know there is a perfectly legal way to get most unpublished telephone numbers? It's right in the voter registration records!

I'll also give you some hints as to which documents are most valuable for certain background checks, which should help you reduce your time, effort, and expense. But remember to watch for new sources of information, never confining your efforts to a selected set of documents just to save time and money. The one information source you skip may contain just the facts you are looking for.

WHY YOU NEED OBJECTIVE INFORMATION

To be successful in your search, you must learn how to develop your own information on a particular person, and that information must be reliable. There is just too much hard data available, as well as services that can assist you inexpensively, for you ever to rely only upon your instincts.

What happens all too often, particularly in major fraud cases, employee theft, or "rent and run" cases, is that employers, credit managers, landlords, and prospective spouses rely too heavily on the data supplied by the subject of their search. They put too much emphasis on interviews and the person's résumé, financial statement, and references.

You should always be aware that at least a third of all résumés contain false information. Of course, some of that is harmless, but how can you decide what is really important?

Watch out for financial statements. As illustrated by recent bank fraud scandals and failures, they often aren't worth the paper they are printed on.

Personal references are almost always chosen by the job applicant, so if that person is a fraud, you had better not depend on those references, because they could even be an integral part of the scam. You also need to know about the emerging new business of reference services that provide false information. You pay them a fee, and they verify any facts you ask them to.

Sylvia Johnson (not her real name, as this and most other names in this book have been changed) is a prime example of reference falsification. She runs a personnel scam. For $20 she will give you a number you can use as a personal or business reference where she will respond to any type of employer questions, telling the unsuspecting caller that you are a wonderful person and a fine human being.

Sylvia is a pro. Her phone is answered, "Good morning! May I help you?" When you ask for a specific company name, she says, "Yes, this is [the company]." Sylvia knows all the tricks.

She will not volunteer any information about the reference but will verify whatever the interviewer asks her. She knows most employers don't expect her to offer information, but to verify the applicant's comments, because

5

that is most companies' policy. Besides, Sylvia, who has a growing business, does so many of these she couldn't possibly remember them all.

How do you protect yourself from someone like Sylvia? Check on one or two items out of context, or give her a piece of false information inconsistent with the material supplied by the applicant. If your probe comes back verified (such as verifying prior employment in Dallas, but a residence in another town over 200 miles away), then red flags should go up about the integrity of her verification.

Another trick is to call the same number and ask for another company. See if Sylvia verifies that too. You'd be amazed at how many Sylvias there are out there verifying résumé information.

No matter how effective you believe you are in making character decisions, interviews leave you open to smooth-talking con artists just waiting to win their game by encouraging you to trust them because of their charisma, charm, and wit. Securing your trust through interviews, thus preempting proper background screens, is a potent weapon for successful cons.

By accepting and depending on facts provided by subjects themselves, you are depriving yourself of the one tool needed to make sound decisions or to protect yourself: *objective and balanced information from verifiable sources.*

HOW TO START A PROPER BACKGROUND CHECK

Before you initiate any background or public records investigation, set up a checklist, a list of specific records and information you intend to research. No professional investigator ever embarks on a background check without this list. A checklist of the records you intend to search assures that you don't overlook any vital source, keeps you or others assisting you from duplicating efforts, and helps organize incoming information, which can get out of hand if you aren't careful.

The form on page 9 is an example of a checklist of records used by many investigators. It will help you organize your background search, so either use it or study the concept and design your own according to your needs.

Identify Whom You're Investigating

Your first step in a public records search is to properly identify the person you are investigating. Don't be fooled by the obviousness of the basic identifying information you have been given. Remember, it may be false!

Often, your biggest problem in any investigation is that the identifying information you have been given is incorrect, an outright lie, or incomplete. In fact, the basic facts may be the very information you are trying to document through public records before you can continue your search. How do you determine which public records are most likely to fill in the blanks on the identifying information? Here's a hint that will help guide you in your search for valid identifying information: *be careful and think specifics.*

For example, suppose you're the owner of commercial property you are about to lease to a new tenant. The person who contacts you says his name is Bob Smith. Ask him whether his full name is Bob or Robert. Does he use or have a middle initial? Ask the same questions of anyone who uses a nickname.

If you are dealing with a principal or agent of a company or are planning to enter into an agreement with a business, you'll need to ask for even more information.

Obtain Other Identifying Information

Depending on the situation that prompted you to run your search, obtain any other identifying information you can. For example, when hiring someone, it's sensible to ask for a driver's license number, because this is a frequently used source of identification. When you believe it is appropriate, push for as much data as you can get.

Don't ignore your own senses either. Jot down on the identifying form on the following page what you hear or observe. For example, when you see the subject's car, record the license plate number. (Guess how many fathers do that with their daughters' first dates!)

Don't ever worry that you are being too suspicious. You are merely being careful and specific. Once you get into the habit, the rest comes naturally.

Put the Pieces Together

Finally, weave the web. Assemble the pieces of the puzzle, and make sense of the varied information you get from public records. The information is all there, but you must learn to view it in the proper perspective in order to analyze it and learn to understand what it means in the aggregate. Here's an example.

On paper, Jerry Ewing was a great engineer with excellent credentials, good schools, and glowing recommendations from supervisors. Why then did he move every year, having five employers in four states in as many years? Was he merely upwardly mobile, following his chosen ca-

BACKGROUND/RECORDS RESEARCH FORM

CASE # _____ INV _____

SUBJECT_____ SPOUSE _____

VOTER REGISTRATION	MARRIAGE LICENSE
Name _____	Husband Name _____
_____	Address _____
Address _____	_____
City/Zip _____	City/Zip _____
DOB _____	Proof of ID _____
SS# _____	DOB _____
Phone # _____	SS# _____
	Phone # _____

TELEPHONE DIRECTORY	Wife Name _____
Name _____	Address _____
_____	_____
Address _____	_____
Phone # _____	Proof of ID _____
Comments _____	DOB _____
_____	SS#_____

PUBLIC UTILITIES	PUBLIC UTILITIES
Name _____	Name _____
_____	_____
Address _____	Address _____
_____	_____
City/Zip _____	City/Zip _____
SS# _____	SS# _____
Phone # _____	Phone # _____
Comments _____	Comments _____
_____	_____

reer path? Nope. He had an ex-wife three states back trying to nail him for child support. So in order to stay ahead of the constable and his ex, who tracked his wages from state to state trying to recover the thousands of dollars Jerry owed her and his children, Jerry had to move each year when his employer filed his tax information. As far as I know, Jerry is still running, moving from job to job, one step ahead of the law. One of these days, he is going to have to slow down or change his identity to avoid the warrants for his arrest that follow him wherever he goes.

THE RECORDS

All right, now that you've got the basic idea, let's start our search. We'll begin with voter registrations.

Voter Registration

Voter registration records are the single best information source for locating people and their addresses. You can use these registrations to find missing persons, delinquent debtors, long-lost cousins, or a wealth of new data on your subject of investigation. Voter registration information is crucial to almost all my background checks, no matter what their purpose.

Let's look at the information available to you on a voter registration card and what it can do for you:

- *Name*—A voter registration is one of the likeliest places someone will use a full and correct legal name as well as the names of his or her spouse and voting-age children.

- *Current address, or address for the most recent election*—The voter must give the registrar a valid mailing address because the voter won't receive the card necessary for voting eligibility if it cannot be delivered to a good mailing address. *Voter registrations are canceled when returned from an undeliverable address.*

- *Past addresses from former elections*—I have been able to trace people through numerous addresses for over twenty years using voter registration applications that list the address of the subject and a year he or she was there.

- *Age and date of birth*—Because of legal age requirements for voting, a voter must state his or her age and date of birth on the voter application. Oddly, I've found that some of the most notorious cons, people who wouldn't tell the truth if you put a gun to their head, often state their correct age and date of birth on a voter registration form, never realizing that an astute investigator can trace them through this source.

- *Social Security number*—Though listing Social Security numbers on voter registrations is optional, many people add them anyway, just because the form asks them to. The Social Security number is the one identifier that will be most instrumental in finding the place your subject grew up and where he or she is working and spending money. (See the section about Social Security numbers later in this chapter.)

- *Signatures*—Voting authorities require voters to sign their registration forms as they must sign any other official document. Investigators needing signature samples can compare those from voter registrations with questionable documents such as checks or money orders that a con swears never to have signed or forged.

As you can see, information on voter registrations can really help you positively identify the subject of your background check—your first step in every investigative process. Even if you thought you already had all the information provided by the registration, a check will help you corroborate it, which is especially valuable if the data were provided by your subject and not verified through documentation.

If you find any data on your subject's voter registration that disagree with what the person told you, you should recognize that something is wrong and search even harder until you think you've learned the whole truth.

How to Examine Voter Registrations Most major counties in the nation now have computerized voter registrations or sell the lists on microfilm or microfiche for a nominal initial charge, providing updated rolls annually for a small fee. You can find out the costs by contacting the office of the county clerk in your jurisdiction.

Getting a list of registered voters is easy and inexpensive. However, there are times when you might need to examine the registration application itself to get the most out of voter registrations.

One of the little-known secrets in our trade is that when you need the unlisted telephone number of an individual, you can often find it in voter registrations. Many jurisdictions ask voters to write their telephone number on the front or back of the application form. Most individuals, especially those who would never give their number anywhere else, do just that—and make your day.

Here's how a smart investigator applies this knowledge: Go to the courthouse and ask the records clerk to show you the actual registration application, telling him or her you need to check a signature on a voter's card. Once you have the card, find the telephone number and write it down. You may need to turn the card over from the signature side, but do so discreetly, and you will have the information you need. Of course, if you really do need to check the subject's signature, you can do that as well.

Stretching Voter Registration Data You may wonder about the overall benefit of going to voter registrations for most of your background checks, considering that so few people vote. Often, someone who wants to keep publicly available personal information to a minimum will use a voter registration card as a means of identification. This is especially true of illegal aliens. (Yes, many illegal aliens are registered to vote.) These people often need their voter registration identification card to cash checks at the supermarket or a local check-cashing service. Whatever the reason, many people do it, and information that everywhere else they lie about or hide they are likely to put accurately on the voter application.

Even if a person doesn't vote or rarely votes, it may not be a problem, because he or she may still be registered. In every county in the nation, vast organizations are formed to bring out the vote, identify persons able to vote, and get them registered to vote. Even if the subject of your check isn't registered, it is quite possible that his or her spouse, or a son or daughter, is registered as a voter at the same address. So when you find the spouse or a person with the same last name listed (especially if it's an unusual name), you know that you're probably tracking down the people you want.

For months I had been trying to locate a real estate agent, Maria Pultz, to serve her court papers that would legally require her to appear as a crucial witness in a case. Maria ran a small real estate business through telephone advertisements and an answering service and used a post office box for all her mail. Consequently, no one interested in the case had an actual street address on Maria, so they could not serve papers on her. However, Maria's last name was unique.

A search of voter registrations showed only one person with that same last name who was registered. That person turned out to be Maria's daughter, who had used her mother's home address, rather than her college dorm, which changed every year. When Maria was served, her only comment was a shocked "How on earth did you find me?" She still doesn't know her daughter was unknowingly our snitch.

Thus, never assume you're through once you have searched the lists of voters, even if you don't find your subject listed as a registered voter. If you find that your subject's spouse or children have registered to vote, you have the address you need, or at least the names of other family members who can lead you to the information about the people you really want.

Marriage Licenses

To paraphrase a great philosopher, "I love a wedding." Weddings provide us with a wealth of identifying data in our quest for information.

14

On the surface, marriage licenses and the primary information they provide—that is, that two people have recorded their union—might not seem to be too valuable for general background checks or for complex cases such as asset searches or verifications. It may seem that way, but don't you believe it! Marriage licenses are extremely valuable general-purpose documents for background researchers, especially for the following objectives:

- Developing identifying information

- Locating individuals

- Locating family members

- Finding new pathways to search for information

Consider the objective of finding new pathways to search for information as the real key to using marriage licenses. When you are using marriage licenses and other public records, always remember that *you are working a process as well as using a product*. The documents are important not only because of what they tell you about your subject now but also for where the information contained in those documents might lead you to find other data you are ultimately searching for.

Where to Find Marriage Licenses A large part of the value of marriage licenses to investigators lies in their near universality. Almost everyone at some point falls in heat or in love and feels the urge to get married and to record that fact.

Marriage licenses are filed in the county courthouse of the legal residence of the married couple at the time of the marriage, or in state records that are usually filed at the department of vital statistics.

In itself, knowing how and where to look for marriage licenses may pose your most serious problem. For example, Las Vegas considers a person a resident after only three days and will then grant a quickie marriage license. You may also be looking for someone who has moved frequently since his or her marriage or whose wedding date you do not know. However, these problems are not as complex as they may appear at first glance.

Though Las Vegas is often believed to be something of a marriage mecca, not that many couples actually get married there. As for the frequent movers, you can find their previous addresses in the other identifying information sources already described in this chapter and thereby have an idea or two about where your subject has been. Another possibility is searching the county where the parties were issued their Social Security numbers (more on Social Security numbers later in this chapter).

What You Can Learn What information will you find on the marriage license? Here are the basics:

- *Full legal names of the couple*—Again, this is most important in fully developing identifying information. Another important item is the full maiden name of the woman being married. The name you are looking for may have changed through marriage.
- *Dates of birth*
- *Social Security numbers*
- *Permanent address of the couple at the time of marriage*

16

- *Other identifying information*—In the case of U.S. nationals, marriage licenses usually include a driver's license number. In the case of foreign nationals, a passport often is used as identification and is the best way for you to trace your subject to his or her land of birth.

- *Prior marriages*—Many jurisdictions ask if either of the partners has been married previously, and list the other names the spouse has used.

- *Witnesses*—Although the witnesses at weddings who sign the marriage certificate may have nothing to do with the couple, often they are the best friends of one of the parties, so they will have known that person all his or her life and can tell you a lot.

Where the Information Might Lead You The value of a marriage license is not so much what it contains as where it can lead you. The first three items mentioned—legal names, dates of birth, and Social Security numbers—are self-explanatory. This document can help you fill in information you might not have, such as the maiden name of a woman, which you can use to track her history and possibly discover valuable information that corroborates what you already know.

But what about the addresses of the couple at the time of the wedding? Let's say, for example, you were having problems locating your subject. If the marriage partners were young when they got married, those addresses were probably those of their parents. Following up on that address may open up information about high schools, or could put you in contact with a yearbook or possibly a reunion committee. Often reunion committees are great sources for locating people who move frequently. One investigator I know uses the pretext that he is on a reunion committee and contacts parents, trying to locate their child—a good way to approach parents he might have found through the addresses contained in the marriage license.

There are many other ways you can use this kind of information. For example, one day, one of my female investigators was having her hair done at a beauty salon and heard the most tragic love story of her life. The beautician, after hearing that Diane was a private investigator and located people for a living, told the investigator how she had been looking for her first love for over forty-five years and how finding him was the only thing she now lived for.

Sherry had grown up with George and had been his steady in high school. He gave her his class ring just before he joined the army and went overseas to fight in World War II. She wrote to him all through basic training, saw him off on the troop ship leaving for England, and then never saw him again.

After several years, with no letters and no word from her high school sweetheart, Sherry married another boy and moved to Texas, believing that George had been killed in the war or possibly had found a new love over there. As the years passed, she kept the pictures of George, reread his letters, and wondered what had happened to the life they had planned.

When her husband died, eight years ago, Sherry decided that she was going to make every effort to look for George in the hope that he too might be widowed, divorced, or at least alive so that she could see him once again. She went back to her old hometown, called her high school friends, and drove up and down the street that George had lived on, hoping to find someone who knew what had happened to him and where he had gone. For eight years she tried every means she knew, spent every vacation hour and probably a good deal of the money she had put away for retirement, on his trail. Still, all of Sherry's efforts were in vain; she just couldn't find anyone who knew what had happened to her George.

Diane was so touched by Sherry's story that she promised to help her in her search. They started by ordering a copy of the high school yearbook. Then they ordered a driver's license search using George's full name and date of birth. (Sherry had George's birth date inscribed in her heart as well as in the diary she had kept all these years.) The Driver's License Bureau gave an address for 1950, documenting that George was still alive then and had returned home to the county of his birth. Sherry and Diane then convinced the county clerk to go into the attic and search through the musty marriage records, handwritten in the 1940s and 1950s, to see if George had married someone else.

Three days later, the clerk called with news that George had come home and gotten married. From the marriage certificate, the clerk was able to give them a Social Security number and new address. Since this was a small western Pennsylvania county with a small courthouse and public records center, this clerk was also the custodian of the civil suit and divorce records, and he searched these files as well to see if George had divorced his new wife in that county. Through this extra little bit of diligent research, the pair of sleuths found George's divorce file, and in the court pleadings they found his Social Security number and the property settlements in his divorce, which left him in possession of a small farm in an adjoining county.

Once they had the Social Security number and the information about property in another county, it was a simple matter to trace his address through a national credit bureau identifier search and verify through the county tax assessor that he still owned the land.

Two weeks later, Sherry appeared on George's doorstep with the present that he had given her on her eighteenth birthday—a single yellow rose.

I don't know what they said when George opened that door, but I do know he invited her in. They were married three weeks later.

As the case of Sherry illustrates, identifying information—such as a driver's license or passport number—opens other avenues to your search. Driver's license numbers remain essentially the same, even through multiple marriages, and while people don't always change their driver's license addresses when they first move, eventually they have to when their current license expires. For passports the same is true. Remember this: there are vast numbers of foreign nationals out there paying fees ranging from $1,000 to $10,000 to U.S. citizens whom they will then marry just to stay in this country. Find the proxy spouse, and you may find a gold mine of information.

Though indicating a prior marriage may not give you the name of an ex-spouse, at least it informs you the subject has one. That will lead you to explore divorce records and, it is hoped, to find the name of an ex-spouse. No one knows where you are and what you do the way your ex does. An ex will almost always know the former spouse's current address, telephone number, salary, and occupation. If your subject is paying child support (which you can usually learn from the court record of the divorce decree or in the county child support office), the ex will have pertinent information on checking accounts and financial holdings that were partitioned at the time of the divorce.

Another source for finding bank accounts through marriage and divorce records is the records of the county child support office. This division of the county clerk's office will have a record of the bank account number, number of payments made, and a current address on the party paying child support. Why? Because in pending or settled divorce cases, many states require that any child support payments be made to the clerk's office so that the number and amount of payments made can be documented and so that enforcement assistance can be given if the payments aren't made.

Driver's License Records

The photo on a driver's license helped crack the largest embezzlement case ever perpetrated against the Colombian government. When a government audit found that $13 million was missing from Colombia's accounts deposited in Chase Manhattan Bank, investigators directed their suspicions toward a Colombian economic minister who controlled the expenditure and transfer of funds throughout the world, but they had no way of proving that he was part of a plot to defraud his government.

The investigators methodically researched every transaction and found four purchases that were highly suspicious, transactions made by a Houston-based, self-described mercenary who traveled throughout the world. Through our investigation of the foreign travel of this mercenary, we found that deposited checks had cleared his account on June 12, 1985, and that on that date he bought a brand-new Chrysler Imperial for cash, a transaction normally far outside his personal financial power.

With investigators from Colombia and Chase Manhattan Bank, we went to Switzerland and reviewed photographs of all the people who had entered the Swiss bank on that day. (Did you know that most Swiss banks photograph everyone who comes through their doors?) We found that the middleman (the mercenary) was accompanied by our Colombian minister, one of the Colombian army's most trusted generals, and two other high-ranking public officials.

The photo from the driver's license of the middleman enabled us to establish the only physical evidence linking the conspirators directly to the scheme to defraud the Colombian government. This important piece of evidence saved the bank from having to reimburse the Colombian government for millions of dollars; helped prove that a conspiracy had been committed by a vendor, the minister, and his associates; and provided the evidence that convicted all of the parties involved in the crime.

When we confronted the self-made mercenary with the photos and evidence from Switzerland, he said that he would plead guilty to anything, implicate all the other conspirators, and do anything that the government wanted, if he would be put in jail in the United States. He said that if he were sent to Colombia to stand trial, he would never live to see the case come to court. (They play the game a little differently down there.) Before this case came to trial, the judge was murdered, the prosecutor was stabbed sixty-three times and beheaded, and the general was found dead in the jungle. The Colombian minister? He's now in Austria, living well off his share of the $13 million. How do I know? I still get his American Express charges and see the names of the fine restaurants he dines in. As long as he's in Austria, he won't be extradited, but if he ever returns to the United States . . .

Currently forty-six states provide driver's license information as a public record. These states maintain records of driving histories, current addresses, and traffic violations made by the license holders in the state.

You can get such driver's license data from your state's department of public safety or highway patrol. Many states also sell that information to private information resale agencies, which sell it through franchising agreements to investigative agencies, insurance companies, and legitimate employers.

What You'll Find in Driver's License Records One of the great attributes of driver's licenses is the identifying information they contain. That information includes the subject's name, date of birth, and current or recent address.

Also, virtually all states require a photo of the driver on the license. The photo is there to document and establish the driver's visual identity.

How to Use Driver's License Data Driver's licenses are one of the most cost-effective tools for beginning a missing-person's search, once the search has been narrowed to a particular state. If you don't know where to search, the first three digits of a person's Social Security number point to the area or state where the subject grew up and probably got his or her first driver's license. (See the discussion of Social Security numbers later in this chapter.)

Also important in your background or missing-person search is to have the best identifying information you can get. Driver's license data add to your file potentially important characteristics such as date of birth, age, height, weight, hair color, and race. This identifying information can help you corroborate information provided by witnesses and can be purchased by anyone who sends a letter of request and a check to the state licensing agency. A driver's license photo might be the only picture of a subject you'll ever have.

With the license in your possession, you can show the photo to people who may have seen the subject but do not know his or her name and could possibly provide information on the subject's activities or identity.

You may also need to use accident report information and driving records. What would you do if you were sued in an accident that you believed the other party had instigated to make money off you or your insurance company? What if the other driver had a history of causing many such accidents? Accident records and driving records will have the information you need to fight this claim.

Ask any private investigator or insurance adjuster, and he or she will tell you horror stories of people who make a very good living by staging accidents or making up false insurance claims. Here's one of the many such nightmares that our firm has had to deal with:

Bella is a Gypsy—a real one—not the kind you see at a county fair or in a carny sideshow. Her family makes a living staging auto accidents with rental cars—causing minor fender benders with people by stopping short in front of them, sideswiping them on wide turns, and pulling out of blind alleys when they see someone coming.

They can fake an injury better than any Hollywood stuntperson, evoke more sympathy than a TV preacher, and weigh your wallet within two small bills.

Last year, Bella and her family staged numerous auto accidents, made claims for several thefts from her various addresses, and collected thousands of dollars in claims from unsuspecting insurance companies. She even collected thousands of dollars in cash from people who had become the victim of her faked auto accidents and didn't want her claims reported to their insurance companies, either because it would raise their insurance rates or because they didn't have the liability insurance required by law in almost every state. These people gladly pay Bella and her family $500 to $1,000 to forget about their claims.

People like Bella are the worst nightmare of the honest, unsuspecting traveler, who can easily be made to feel that the injury was all his or her fault. Watch out: next time you're driving alone on the road they might find you.

Birth Records

Many people have found illegal ways to obtain birth certificates. One well-known way is to find a deceased person's name in a cemetery, then apply to the state for a copy of the person's birth certificate, saying that it was yours and you lost your copy. As a result, most states no longer allow easy access to birth certificate records or information.

However, there are still ways to get the birth record

information you need. Most states comply with subpoenas or requests from law firms or licensed investigative agencies that present a letter on company stationery stating a valid reason for needing birth information. The same is true if you appear in person, present proper credentials to verify your identity, have a valid reason for searching the birth records, and can specify your reason for wanting the information.

Valid reasons that have persuaded many judges to open files include an attempt to determine a family history of disease, an effort to know the existence of heirs to an estate, and the desire of a once adopted child, now adult, to find his or her true past.

Take, for example, the petitioning of one Judge Holloway. Judge Holloway, a jurist of the old school, believed that sealed files should stay closed. But then a young man came into his court, asking to open his adoption records so he might gain a few more years of life.

In the thirty years of his life, Billy had never known that the people who had raised him weren't his birth parents, but when Billy was diagnosed as having a degenerative bone marrow disease, his parents explained to Billy and the doctor that they could not give the needed tissue for a transplant—they were not his blood relatives and therefore would not be the best donors. Billy and his parents went to Judge Holloway to unseal the court records and find the original name and date of birth of Billy's mother so they could track her down and find a donor who could save Billy's life.

The court records, once unsealed, revealed the name of the birth mother and the identity of the doctor who had attended the birth. With a letter drafted under the judge's signature, the hospital provided the date of birth, address, and parents' names of the birth mother—vital information that led us to her in a matter of hours instead of weeks or months.

To Billy's good fortune, our investigators found that his birth mother had later married the father of her child and borne three more children, whom they kept and raised because the husband was then working and could afford to feed a family. Billy, having been raised as an only child because his adopted mother couldn't have children of her own, now found himself with an extended family and a second blood tie after a successful bone marrow transplant.

Where to Find Birth Records and Why They're Useful In almost all states, birth certificates are maintained by the state's department of vital statistics in the state's capital city. They also are found in the subject's city of birth in the hospital issuing the certificate.

Here are the two major uses for a search of birth records:

1. To help you find other information that can only be found by knowing a person's date of birth. This information can include criminal history and driving history among other facts. Criminal history records are computerized by the arrested party's name and date of birth. The date of birth is added because so many people in the country, or even in the same town, have the same spelling of a name that an additional means of identifying their individuality, such as their date of birth, is needed to be sure that the proper person is charged with a crime. The FBI criminal database, known as the Na-

tional Crime Information Center (NCIC), which collects all criminal data from cities, counties, and states across the country, uses the name and date of birth to record information and query its system.

2. To find information helpful in identifying and locating birth parents of adopted children. The previous example showed how this can work.

Social Security Numbers

According to government surveys, the Social Security number (SSN) is so ingrained in our lives that most Americans find it difficult to believe the system didn't even exist until the 1930s. The numbering system was designed to keep track of the millions of individuals who would be enrolled under the terms of the Social Security Act. Using a nine-digit format, the mechanism allows for the registration of one fewer than a billion persons.

In just over a half century, this number has become a standard identifier for tax returns, bank accounts, driver's licenses, even school records. It has even become the service number assigned to all members of the armed forces.

Most people acquire a Social Security number fairly early in life. In fact, the IRS requires that any child considered a dependent have one by age two, and everyone must have one to begin his or her first job.

Unlike names and addresses, your SSN cannot be duplicated or changed. Ever.

For preemployment screening, obtaining the SSN gives an employer certain benefits; many offices maintaining public or education records are indexed by SSN. With a correct SSN, prospective employers can usually get a broad spectrum of data very useful in evaluating applicants.

Understanding SSNs can also give you clues as to the validity of the applicant's number itself. With the information from this section, you'll be able to spot incorrect or falsified SSNs. We'll give you the information and duplicate the Social Security Administration's handy table that lists assigned SSNs according to state and category.

Breaking the SSN Code Every SSN consists of a similar group of three digits, followed by two, concluding with four. Consecutive zeros within a digit group will never appear. Thus, 000-00-000 is an impossible SSN, as is any combination in which any of the subgroups consists only of zeros.

The first three digits of every SSN constitute the "area" number, indicating the state or territory in which the person was residing when the card was issued. This is a valuable clue to finding school records, old voting records, and some real estate records, usually for the parents of your subjects.

Each state and U.S. territory has been assigned unique area numbers. For example, Texas includes 449 through 467. The more populous the state, the greater the number of area prefixes.

With job applicants, once you know the area prefix, you can spot inconsistencies in applications. For instance, if a person claims to be from Georgia and has an SSN prefix that indicates the number was assigned in California, yet there's no history of California employment, that's your cue to ask why the card was issued there. The answer may be quite innocent—college, service in the armed forces, many other perfectly legitimate reasons—but still, it's worth a follow-up. And the answer may not turn out to be innocent after all.

Also keep in mind that not all the possible area prefixes have been assigned to date. These are the only current SSN area prefixes:

001 through 587
589 through 626
700 through 728

Any claimed SSN with an area prefix other than these cannot be valid. The table at the end of this chapter lists the actual prefixes for each state and territory.

The second two digits, together called the "group number," are another key for spotting false or erroneous SSNs. The group number breaks down SSNs in specific areas into more manageable blocks. Theoretically, while a group number might be from 01 to 99, many possible groups within the area prefixes have not yet been used. Any claimed SSN with one of those unused group numbers may be assumed to be invalid.

The final four-digit number in each SSN is called the "serial number." It may be any four-digit group from 0001 to 9999. The serial number reveals an SSN's numerical position within a group. Remember, the only invalid serial number is 0000. All other combinations are OK.

How to Use the SSN Table To check an SSN against the table on pages 32–35, simply find the appropriate area number in column (1), then read across the group columns to make sure the area-group combination you have been given is possible. For example, suppose a job applicant supplied 510-08-1234 as his SSN. In the first column, you'll find that the area number falls in the 509 to 515 range, which is currently being assigned. However, notice in column (4) that no even group number lower than 10 has been issued yet, so this SSN cannot be valid.

In column (6), you can match each area number to its assigned state or territory. If an applicant with SSN 540-09-1234 tells you she's lived in Florida all her life, you have a right to be suspicious. While this *is* a valid number, it could only have been issued to an Oregon resident. You may want to check on this one.

If another Florida applicant supplies an SSN of 590-72-2222, a glance at column (6) verifies this is a valid Florida prefix. However, column (3) tells you the group number 72 is too high to be correct, because the highest even group number greater than or equal to 10 for that area is 60. This number is invalid.

Yet another applicant says her SSN is 627-66-1234. Column (1) reveals that area number 627 is still unassigned. No SSNs with this prefix have ever been issued, so this one is invalid, too.

Use the table a few more times, and you'll quickly see what a good investigative device it is—and it's quite a time saver, too.

SOCIAL SECURITY NUMBER TABLE

(1)	(2)	(3)	(4)	(5)	(6)

Highest Group Numbers

Area Number	Odd less than 10	Even 10 and Above	Even less than 10	Odd greater than 10	State or Territory
000	None	None	None	None	Unassigned
001	09	74	None	None	New Hampshire
002–003	09	72	None	None	New Hampshire
004	09	86	None	None	Maine
005–007	09	84	None	None	Maine
008	09	70	None	None	Vermont
009	09	68	None	None	Vermont
010–029	09	68	None	None	Massachusetts
030–034	09	66	None	None	Massachusetts
035–037	09	56	None	None	Rhode Island
038–039	09	54	None	None	Rhode Island
040–041	09	82	None	None	Connecticut
042–049	09	80	None	None	Connecticut
050–119	09	72	None	None	New York
120–134	09	70	None	None	New York
135–152	09	82	None	None	New Jersey
153–158	09	80	None	None	New Jersey
159–184	09	68	None	None	Pennsylvania
185–211	09	66	None	None	Pennsylvania
212–216	09	98	08	17	Maryland
217–220	09	98	08	15	Maryland
221–222	09	72	None	None	Delaware
223–228	09	98	08	45	Virginia
229–231	09	98	08	43	Virginia
232	09	98	08	33	North Carolina West Virginia
233–234	09	98	08	33	West Virginia
235–236	09	98	08	31	West Virginia
237–246	09	98	08	55	North Carolina
247–248	09	98	08	71	South Carolina
249–251	09	98	08	69	South Carolina
252–258	09	98	08	61	Georgia
259–260	09	98	08	59	Georgia

32

(1)	(2)	(3)	(4)	(5)	(6)
		Highest Group Numbers			
Area Number	*Odd less than 10*	*Even 10 and Above*	*Even less than 10*	*Odd greater than 10*	State or Territory
261–267	09	98	08	99	Florida
268–272	09	88	None	None	Ohio
273–302	09	86	None	None	Ohio
303–309	09	98	02	None	Indiana
310–317	09	98	None	None	Indiana
318	09	80	None	None	Illinois
319–361	09	78	None	None	Illinois
362–367	09	98	04	None	Michigan
368–386	09	98	02	None	Michigan
387–397	09	98	None	None	Wisconsin
398–399	09	96	None	None	Wisconsin
400–406	09	98	08	33	Kentucky
407	09	98	08	31	Kentucky
408	09	98	08	57	Tennessee
409–415	09	98	08	55	Tennessee
416–424	09	98	08	27	Alabama
425–428	09	98	08	59	Mississippi
429–431	09	98	08	67	Arkansas
432	09	98	08	65	Arkansas
433–438	09	98	08	67	Louisiana
439	09	98	08	65	Louisiana
440–441	09	92	None	None	Oklahoma
442–448	09	90	None	None	Oklahoma
449–463	09	98	08	91	Texas
464–467	09	98	08	89	Texas
468–472	09	98	08	13	Minnesota
473–477	09	98	08	11	Minnesota
478–481	09	98	08	13	Iowa
482–485	09	98	08	11	Iowa
486–490	09	96	None	None	Missouri
491–500	09	94	None	None	Missouri
501	09	98	08	11	North Dakota
502	09	98	08	None	North Dakota
503	09	98	08	13	South Dakota
504	09	98	08	11	South Dakota
505	09	98	08	21	Nebraska

CHECK IT OUT!

(1)	(2)	(3)	(4)	(5)	(6)
		Highest Group Numbers			
Area Number	Odd less than 10	Even 10 and above	Even less than 10	Odd greater than 10	State or Territory
506–508	09	98	08	19	Nebraska
509–515	09	94	None	None	Kansas
516	09	98	08	15	Montana
517	09	98	08	13	Montana
518–519	09	98	08	23	Idaho
520	09	98	08	15	Wyoming
521–524	09	98	08	59	Colorado
525	09	98	08	69	New Mexico
526–527	09	98	08	99	Arizona
528	09	98	08	75	Utah
529	09	98	08	73	Utah
530	09	98	08	27	Nevada
531	09	98	08	None	Washington
532–539	09	98	06	None	Washington
540–544	09	98	08	21	Oregon
545–573	09	98	08	99	California
574*	09	92	None	None	Alaska
575–576	09	98	08	39	Hawaii
577	09	98	08	15	District of Columbia
578–579	09	98	08	13	District of Columbia
580*	09	98	08	21	Puerto Rico Virgin Islands
581–584	09	98	08	99	Puerto Rico
585	09	98	08	67	New Mexico
586*	09	84	None	None	Guam Amer. Samoa N. Mariana Is. Philippines
587	09	98	08	59	Mississippi
588	None	None	None	None	Mississippi
589–591	09	60	None	None	Florida
592–595	09	58	None	None	Florida
596–597	09	14	None	None	Puerto Rico
598–599	09	12	None	None	Puerto Rico

(1)	(2)	(3)	(4)	(5)	(6)
		Highest Group Numbers			
Area Number	*Odd less than 10*	*Even 10 and Above*	*Even less than 10*	*Odd greater than 10*	State or Territory
600	09	50	None	None	Arizona
601	09	48	None	None	Arizona
602–620	03	None	None	None	California
621–626	01	None	None	None	California
627–699	None	None	None	None	Unassigned
700–723	09	18	None	None	RR Retirement**
724	09	28	None	None	RR Retirement**
725–726	09	18	None	None	RR Retirement**
727	09	10	None	None	RR Retirement**
728	09	14	None	None	RR Retirement**
729–999	None	None	None	None	Unassigned

*SSNs in these areas also assigned to Southeast Asian refugees during period from April 1975 through November 1979.
**No longer issued.

2

WHOSE BUSINESS IS IT?

One of the most serious problems you may encounter in business today is the professional con artist who moves to the area of the country where business is most active. He was in Texas in 1983, moved to New England in 1985, Atlanta in 1988. Guess where he's going next?

The biggest frauds are most often executed by the razzle-dazzle con artist who has come in as the new business partner or financier of an established local business. This "equity partner" seeks to convince you of his or her class status by displaying flashy diamond rings and gold designer watches, and by treating you to the finest restaurants in town. This smooth-talking devil delivers a great sales pitch and produces a voluminous but vague financial statement, listing assets in unfunded public shells or business ventures that value his or her personal holdings in millions of dollars. The professional con artist tries to sell you the sizzle, not the steak.

You can protect yourself from these unscrupulous types by doing some thorough checking. Each county and state has a system for registering businesses, whether corporations, joint ventures, sole proprietorships, or partnerships. Government agencies do this for tax purposes and so businesses can protect the names of their companies. States and counties also keep on file registered assumed names, known as "doing business as" files (DBAs), which contain lists of businesses operating under a name other than their known business name. These files are a company's means of legally protecting its names from other parties who might want to use that same name.

Remember, a company may be registered with a state and not a county, and vice versa. There is no good rule of thumb to determine where a person may have registered except this: all corporations are chartered by the state, and most partnerships, joint ventures, and sole proprietorships will be registered by either the state or the county.

Corporate charter information is kept by the secretary of state's office in most states. If not, you can request it from the department that handles corporate record information. At the county level, ask for the county clerk's assumed-name or DBA department. Many of these records are now easy to acquire from information resellers such as Prentice-Hall Legal and Financial Services or Information America, companies that specialize in providing on-line public record filings in a growing number of states.

WHAT BUSINESS ENTITY INFORMATION GIVES YOU

Business entity information can confirm that your subject is legally doing business as he or she claims. Anyone can come to you to lease property, contract for goods and services, borrow money, or pursue any other activity (other than opening a bank account). Anyone can have checks, business cards, or letterhead stationery printed that say the person is a principal in a corporation or a partner in a business. The state and county records will reveal whether that's true and if the business has paid its taxes and is in good standing in that jurisdiction.

Here's a little story that illustrates how someone can set up what looks like a business in order to fleece the unsuspecting businessperson: A prisoner in a federal jail, Alan Moore, posed as the president of a major insurance company and almost pulled off a $300 million scam. Moore sent forged documents and letters through the mail and out of prison through parolees to companies seeking brokered business loans. Moore offered insurance policies that claimed to guarantee bank loans through a bonding procedure specified in the loan documents. But the bonds were worth as little as the paper they were printed on, fresh from the prison printing press.

Who got stuck? The people hoping to get the loan. They paid Moore's brokers and agents five to ten thousand dollars each, money that they could ill afford to lose. (That was probably why they got into trouble in the first place.)

Business entity information will also tell you the names of partners, principal shareholders, or board members. Whenever you're doing a background search, gather names of as many of the subject's known associates, family, and friends as you can. They could be the key to vital information, an integral part of any potential wrongdoing, or a source of financial data. (Some naive people think it is really smart to hide their business in their wife's maiden name. I learned that one years ago.)

Finally, you can compile a list of additional business affiliations. Put together a list of other businesses in which the subject may have ownership interests, and compare the partners and corporate officers in the companies. You may find the results very interesting. The list often hints at suspected business affiliations and friends who help hide assets in divorce or judgment proceedings.

IMPORTANCE AND USES OF BUSINESS ENTITY DATA

Breaking Up the Corporate Shell Game

Once you obtain a list of all the corporations or other businesses with which your subject is associated, you are closer to tracing his or her business interests and assets, many of which could be hidden through the old corporate shell game. In this game, a person sets up numerous corporations that transfer funds and assets from one to another, with none of it staying in one place long enough for creditors to collect judgments. A wily corporate crook can use these many corporate entities to draw money from operating businesses or to siphon off money through family or friends.

There are many ways to work this scam, and more are being created every day. Often, the only way to bust this kind of case or to prevent it from spinning you around is to put together a complete list of business affiliations.

Compiling a comprehensive list of your subject's corporate ownerships or checking crossover ownership in multiples of corporations uncovers this scam by revealing the scope of the subject's activities and the corporate vehicles through which the transactions are made. You can often locate and get to the subject's true assets, because you know how he or she has hidden them as well as where and in whose name they have wound up.

This scam is probably how some of the S&L executives made billions of dollars disappear. It explains why the government is having such a tough time finding the money. Through investigating many of the failed banks and savings and loan institutions throughout the United States, I have seen a pattern of fraud and deceit by bankers and customers who create dummy assumed-name companies that act as borrowers and subcontractors to companies getting loans from their institutions.

In one case, a developer borrowed millions of dollars to construct an office building that he convinced the bank was pre-leased by tenants waiting to get into the new offices. The customer presented leases signed by more than a dozen companies promising to fill 70 percent of the office space on the day it was completed.

The bankers, in their rush to make a promising loan and with a little greed in their hearts (because they would get a 20 percent ownership in the building by financing its construction), didn't look closely at the companies signing the leases. If they had, they would have found that these companies were not listed in the phone book, had no business credit rating, and in fact were fictitiously filed into the public record at the courthouse by the developer in his name, his wife's maiden name, and the names of several neighbors on his block. The companies existed only on paper, so they wouldn't be moving anywhere at all.

In due course, the bank gave the developer construction draws totaling 90 percent of the completion price of the building. Thinking they were smart, the bankers wrote the checks to the subcontractors themselves. What they didn't realize was that the developer was one step ahead of them and had created instant subcontractors in assumed-name filings under his wife's maiden name. The developer sent in his expense sheets, the bankers wrote the checks, and the developer cashed them through his wife's "company."

As you may have guessed, the construction was never completed, the tenants never moved in, and today you can drive down the freeway and recognize the vacant status because it's another of those see-through buildings that dot the local landscape.

The bank lost over $20 million on the project and failed in 1990, blaming this loan and several others like it for wiping out its operating capital. The developer simply filed a personal bankruptcy to wipe out his debt. Now he is getting ready to start up a new business in another name, maybe one of those that his wife used so successfully to bilk the bank.

Monitoring Employees and Investigating Theft

In most employee theft cases investigated by our firm, the employees involved had filed assumed names for phony vendor names and were using the names to get payments from their employer or to do business with their employer.

In one case, we discovered that Bob, a man company officials considered to be a rising star and promising young executive, had actually stolen $300,000 by contracting with and double billing his employers through a dummy assumed-name company he had created.

Employers and business owners should also take precautions against vendor theft or collusion between their vendors or clients and their employees. It's a good idea to periodically survey client account lists to verify business trade accounts for credit and documentation purposes.

One of our client company's internal auditors found $400,000 in new sales to a company that was not listed in Dallas's telephone directories and didn't have a listed tax identification number. Investigation of the name and address on the bill indicated that no such corporation was registered in Texas and that the address on the bill was the residence of a purchasing agent of a major supplier.

All checks made to this company were pulled for identification. We found that the checks had been deposited into the account of our own client's purchasing agent or cashed at a liquor store one block from his house. (Could you cash a $40,000 check in a liquor store?)

At a management conference between the two companies, it was verified that the supplier's purchasing agent had transferred the materials to the bogus account, and the materials themselves were shipped to clients. Our client's purchasing agent verified the shipment, cleared the checks for immediate payment, and the two of them split the profits. Both employees were fired, charged with theft, and forfeited over $120,000 of retirement benefits that would have been theirs in the next several years.

Discovering Conflicts of Interest

Conflicts of interest are closely related to employee thefts. Though actual theft may not be involved, many companies, especially without knowledge, do not want their business contracting with employees or executives because the potential for abuses is too great. When checking this out, search for companies or business entities filed in the employee's spouse's name, the wife's maiden name, or their children's names.

Detecting Changes in Financial Status

Checking business entity information can uncover valuable clues to discovering there has been a drastic change in the financial fortunes of your customer. If your subject has dissolved or formed numerous companies, or if your subject has formed new companies with spouse or children as board members, it's a good bet that your subject is trying to hide assets. It is also a good bet that the true nature of your subject's financial condition is not what he or she is making it appear.

A search for substantial changes in financial status can provide especially valuable data for any lender, vendor, or businessperson seeking a partner to bring into his or her business.

PERMITS

Usually, before businesses can open their doors to customers, most municipalities require permits, licenses, and stacks of applications. Cities do that in order to exercise control over certain types of businesses and to generate revenues. Usually, you'll find permits and other applications filed with your city's taxing authority or in the city manager or finance department's offices.

Several other municipal offices require permits and can provide you with valuable data:

- *The fire department* has information if the company stores any kind of chemicals.

- *City environmental departments* are becoming more stringent about monitoring certain types of businesses. In many parts of the country, they now require permits or reviews before certain types of businesses can build or operate.

- *Health departments* require permits for a variety of reasons, including permission for emissions and to allow drainage for certain dangerous or polluting materials.

- *Planning and zoning offices* enforce city regulations that allow only specific or designated classes of businesses to operate in various parts of the city.

Once you've determined the type of business your subject operates, there are probably several municipal jurisdictions and licensing agencies or departments the business will fall under, and you should check them out. The most common permits are for new construction, remodeling, construction site preparation, or for occupational licenses such as those filed with the city health authorities by businesses that prepare food.

Major Uses for Business Permit Data

With business permit data, you may be able to determine the nature of a subject's business. This information can corroborate your subject's statements about his or her current business and whether your subject is even in the business he or she claims to be in. Chances are, people who don't have the proper permits are not in the business that they claim to be.

Business permit data can also help you discover a current location for a business or for your subject. This point is especially significant if your subject lives in a city that charges an occupational license fee. The city taxing authority usually keeps an index of licenses you can use to help you locate any businessperson who tries to keep a step ahead of creditors.

You can use data from permits to corroborate information given to you by prospective tenants or borrowers. Searching business permit records is an integral part of your continuing effort to determine the true activities of anyone attempting to borrow money or the background of someone who wants to lease your property. Remember that anyone can claim to be in business and get letterhead and business cards printed. Searching for relevant permits that authorize your subject to conduct the business he or she claims to be in can tell you if the subject actually is in that business and therefore has a legitimate need to receive financing or a lease.

UNIFORM COMMERCIAL CODE (UCC) RECORDS

If you want to find the bank account or the company financing a subject's daily business operations, then consult the records of UCC filings. Uniform Commercial Code (UCC) records or financing statements are documents that indicate the interest a lending institution has in an asset being used as collateral for a loan. Frequently banks, finance companies, retailers, and other commercial creditors file a UCC statement with the county or state to make public their security interest in assets that have been pledged as collateral. The filing is intended to prevent other parties from claiming an interest in those assets.

The assets most often secured by UCC filings are boats, large appliances, business equipment, and leased equipment where the equipment is the asset and collateral for the loan. These filings are most often used to record security for personal or business loans and office or equipment leases.

Finance companies that loan money regularly file UCCs to secure publicly the purchase of color televisions, refrigerators, washers and dryers, and other purchases made by customers who don't pay cash but finance the payments with credit from the finance companies.

Where to Find UCCs

Generally, UCCs are filed with the county and state—for counties, in the county clerk's office; for states, with the secretary of state or in the commercial department of the state records office. Whenever you visit either of these offices, just ask for all the UCCs filed on your specific subject, by name.

These records are also found on-line through firms such as Information America, Dun and Bradstreet, and Prentice-Hall Legal and Financial Services.

How UCCs Can Aid Your Background Checks

Finding Out Where Your Subject Banks To say UCCs can help you in asset searches would understate the value of these filings as well as the importance of identifying your subject's banking relationships. Any good investigator will tell you that the key to finding out whether there are potential problems with a subject is directly related to whether or not you can find the subject's money. If you can't, chances are you are dealing with someone who deserves further scrutiny, that something about him or her isn't exactly legitimate.

Locating the banks your subject deals with is an important step in any search. If you can't find a subject's bank or can't even determine whether the subject has any bank at all, then how does he or she transact business? Is your subject hiding the business he or she transacts by dealing only in cash or through a hidden or private source? If that is the case, why is the subject transacting business in that manner?

On the other hand, finding that the subject has a bank and knowing which bank that is gives you a source to contact about how the subject handles accounts and conducts business with the banks using those accounts. Bankers can tell you whether the subject has a good relationship with them and if the subject's financial position is as represented.

Uncovering Clues About Financial Position That's not all, though. Identifying banking relationships and contacting banks can ultimately reveal where a subject's money is going, if it's going where the subject says it is going, and perhaps if there are places it's going that the subject may not have told you about (for example, child support or to the IRS). When you locate a subject's banks, you are closing in on finding out about unusual changes of financial condition. Whatever the case, identifying a subject's banks opens a whole world of information and other possibilities for your search.

Another point to watch for is whether there are many recent filings, especially if you are a potential lender or prospective business partner of the subject's. You might compare the subject's position in his or her financial statement against a large list of UCC filings on the subject to determine if the financial statement is accurate and current or if the subject has experienced any significant changes, particularly downturns, in financial condition.

"Skip Tracing" and Finding New Leads To drum up new business when I first became an investigator, I would visit lawyers and ask them to try me out on their oldest, dirtiest, nastiest cases, the ones nobody wanted or had been able to crack. If I could deliver what they needed, then they would pay me. If I wasn't successful, no fee.

I once made this proposition to a New Orleans lawyer who was on the lookout for a "sucker" like me. That attorney, whose client was a large insurance company, had a three-year-old fraud case that had gone nowhere, and the trial was a scant thirty days away.

The lawyer's only lead was a witness who had reported seeing the subject, a man named Jim Snow, driving a tractor over the slab of a burned-out building. The attorney believed Snow had been hired to crack the slab so the building's fire loss would be 100 percent.

The problem: no one could locate the elusive Jim Snow. He was known to be a somewhat shady character who usually worked small construction jobs on a day-to-day basis for cash.

My initial record check turned up little, but there was a two-year-old UCC filed by Beneficial Finance Company, your friendly neighborhood lender. Beneficial, like many lenders, keeps a computerized record of its borrowers to track their loans and their credit history.

I called Beneficial's New Orleans office, posing as the manager of a new finance company, and asked the manager about Jim Snow. Beneficial's manager told me the company didn't have any current business with Mr. Snow, but that he had paid off his loan over a year ago. However, he did mention that a copy of Snow's file had been sent on to Beneficial's office near Richmond, Virginia, at Snow's request. When I asked why, the manager said evidently Mr. Snow had moved there and was taking out another loan and wanted his good payment history to follow him to his new address.

With that information in hand, I again used the role of new credit manager and called Beneficial in Richmond, Virginia, where I obtained Snow's new address. That was on Friday.

Monday, after only three days' part-time effort, I presented the lawyer with my information and asked, "Would you like me to get his statement?"

The attorney was stunned. The first thing he asked was how I found Snow. My reply: "You paid me to find him, not to tell you how."

Through my efforts, I gathered two new clients whom I still have today—the lawyer and the insurance company.

Here's a little secret for you: finance companies are usually willing to share information about their borrowers, especially if the borrower is past due or has skipped out on a loan. Also, these lenders run some of the best skip tracers in the country. Through their night owls, who track down bad accounts after the sun goes down, you can often find new leads or new addresses.

3

SEE YOU IN COURT

CRIMINAL HISTORIES

An apparently pervasive opinion in the United States is that criminal records and histories are confidential. They're not. Almost all criminal history information is open to public scrutiny. You just have to know where to look.

There are a few criminal records that are not available to the public, however. These include state and federal databases of criminal information such as the NCIC (National Crime Information Center), which are not considered public domain records. The unauthorized acquisition and/or use of these confidential police information databases carries severe penalties. The records are confidential because they often contain classified material on continuing investigations and about informants, and police agencies hoard this information, keeping it even from each other.

Where to Find Criminal Records

The best places to start your search for criminal histories filed at the city, county, or state level are the county or district clerk and criminal division. Federal charges are filed with the federal clerk's office at your neighborhood federal building.

Other sources you can contact include the municipal court clerk, city police, county sheriff, county constable, probation office, state police, the state offices supervising probation and parole, the U.S. marshal, bail bondsmen, county jails, and the prison locater service in your state.

Some of these sources can be particularly valuable if you already know your subject's criminal status. For example, if you know the person is on probation, finding and talking to his or her probation officer is usually the best means of getting "in touch" with your subject. If your subject was or is in prison, the prison locater service can tell you where the subject is or how, when, and where he or she was released. To locate a prisoner, you will need a full legal name and a Social Security number.

How to Use Criminal Records and Histories

For some reason, most honest people who aren't used to them find it difficult to grub around in criminal records. Maybe it makes them feel sleazy or just uncomfortable to be so close to the criminal element. Force yourself, though—for two reasons. First, even though most subjects won't have criminal records, the one who does could truly make your life miserable. Second, you can achieve peace of mind.

Obviously, criminal histories can be important, but as

you'll discover about other records, you may find a broader application for them than you originally expected. Criminal records from other investigations can help you locate assets, find missing persons, and identify the subject's known friends and associates. They'll reveal trends through prior charges and demonstrate the operating methods, or modus operandi (M.O.), a subject might use. And whenever you spot a subject with a criminal history, that takes you into a whole new constellation of information availability.

What You Can Expect to Find in Criminal Records

The following list names exhibits you might find in a criminal clerk's files on your subject. Not all of these exhibits will be in every defendant's file, but you should watch for them:

- Criminal charge
- Indictment statement
- Pretrial information report
- Conviction statement
- Incarceration information

If the subject was convicted, records will indicate where the person has been remanded, as well as his or her ultimate destination—county jail or state or federal prison. His or her sentence and information regarding parole or probation eligibility, fines, penalties, and any restitution ordered by the court or jury should also appear in the criminal clerk's files.

Probation Information Sometimes a person charged and convicted of a crime is granted probation or a reduced term of incarceration in conjunction with an extended probation. Included in the probation records are terms and conditions of the probation established by the court. These may include restitution, fines, community service requirements the convicted person must perform, any treatment for psychological or chemical addiction disorders, the reporting jurisdiction and schedule, geographic limitations of work and travel, and circumstances under which the probationer will lose the probation and must serve jail time. Also included in the file may be pertinent personal information on the probationer that may affect the terms of the probation. That information may cover living conditions, employment, marital status, health data, and even financial condition.

Pretrial Information Criminal records cover pretrial interviews with the defendant, including the defendant's personal history and employment history, as well as prior criminal charges and typical physical identifying information on the defendant and any other parties charged with the crime. This is the best source for uncovering previous charges and convictions, because defendants often admit the actual history in the pretrial information interview.

Information on Bail-Bonding Agencies No one knows more about a defendant than the person who makes the defendant's bond. While holding that bond, the bondsman is closer to a defendant than his or her family until the bondsman's client shows up in court.

To secure the bond money, a bail-bonding agency often gets more information than the police and frequently requires the defendant or family members to deposit or pledge sufficient assets to secure the full face amount of a bond before writing it. If a defendant skips out on bond, the agency shares a common interest with you in locating the defendant. The information the agency has can be valuable in locating the defendant as well as the defendant's family and friends.

By taking the information from the bail-bonding agency and comparing it against the defendant's criminal file, the investigator can often identify the relationship between the people the defendant has listed as friends, relatives, or references, and find out from the agency whether it has represented any of them as well. In most cases, people are referred to bail-bonding agencies by others who have used their services in the past, so there's a good chance that the people listed as references both to the bondsman and to the court have a criminal history of their own, which you can examine to find out more about your subject as well.

Other Information Finally, the criminal court file can offer other data pertaining to the victim's financial restitution and the perpetrator's probation, parole, and incarceration, from the county jail to "Club Fed." (I once interviewed Vincent, a prisoner at Egland Air Force Base, Florida, a minimum-security federal prison, to determine some arcane bit of information on a federal case. When I called in to Vincent, I was told he couldn't see me until three o'clock because he was the third chair on the prison tennis team and was in a match. No wonder they call that place "Club Fed.")

It makes me chuckle every time I think of Egland

because the first case that I worked on as a federal agent was the investigation of Myer Lansky and his lawyer, who were sentenced to this same "Club Fed." When I first saw this attorney, he had a heart condition, was a chronic alcoholic, and had bags under his eyes that you could pack clothes in. A year later, when I went to interview him regarding another aspect of the Lansky investigation, I saw to my amazement that he was a new man. In the year at prison, the attorney had dried out from his alcohol problems, dropped four strokes from his golf game, and developed a healthy Florida tan. I'll bet we added ten years to his life by sending him to the state "spa" and making him follow a diet without booze.

CIVIL SUITS—THE PEOPLE'S COURT

Most of us never become part of the criminal records system because we're not charged with a crime. But almost everyone has been a plaintiff, witness, or defendant in a civil case of some type. We sue or get sued over traffic accidents, bad debts, divorces, or conflicts arising from our employment.

Civil litigation records are a wellspring of information, regardless of the particular reason you are running a search. Checking these records is an absolute must anytime you conduct a background search.

It seems strange to me that whenever a police officer wants to locate information on a suspect, he or she usually goes first to criminal records, looking for previous charges. What if the suspect has never been charged or caught? Most law enforcers don't even know civil court records exist, and fewer know how to use them properly.

Unfortunately for police officers looking for criminals

in existing records, only one in twenty citizens is listed in the records of the National Crime Information Center. In fact, government records show that for every individual charged in a criminal case, at least ten are involved in some sort of civil suit. So your chances of finding someone in civil suits are ten times greater than in criminal records.

In the civil suit records, you can discover, recorded for posterity, the true feelings of ex-spouses, business associates, and those dirty bastards who owe us money—or to whom we owe money. Civil suits are filed at the city, county, state, and federal levels. Most often, they are filed to collect debts or damages, to dissolve relationships, to answer claims of civil rights abuses, to obtain civil damage awards against people, or to settle matters that do not violate criminal statutes in any specific way.

Where Do You Find Court Records?

Civil suit records cover different issues according to the courts involved:

- *Municipal and small-claims courts*—Minor financial matters, usually with a low dollar limit on the claim (an amount varying with jurisdiction), such as hot checks, nonpayment of small debts, and restitution for minor damages, are filed with municipal and county small-claims courts. These suits are settled by a justice of the peace.

- *District and superior state courts*—Suits for larger financial damages, personal injury, divorce, and other civil matters seeking substantial damages or requiring complex discovery, action, and litigation are filed in these higher courts. They are settled by a judge or jury.

57

- *Federal District Court*—These courts hear matters involving interstate commerce or principals who live or operate in separate states, antitrust issues, civil rights cases, international business and personal relations, conflicts involving contracts with the federal government, problems involving federally chartered financial institutions, and a host of other federally related conflicts.

Because of the complexity involved in the federal and state court cases, their records are usually extensive and informative. You'll find depositions pertinent to the backgrounds of all the parties, addresses and names of witnesses written on subpoenas, and citations served on the parties involved. Claims of all types are thoroughly laid out to prove civil damages.

Depositions are legalized fishing expeditions where an attorney gets to ask the person being deposed about his or her background, current activities, and any facts that the lawyer deems pertinent to the case at hand. The object of taking a deposition is to get an answer to all the questions that may be asked in court so that there will be no surprises in the courtroom. Through depositions attorneys hope to find the weak spot in a client's case or find areas that they are better off staying away from in order to avoid incriminating their own client. A trial lawyer has no greater fear than to ask a witness a question that the lawyer doesn't know the answer to and have that answer delivered to a packed courtroom as it so often was in the Perry Mason thrillers.

Types of Actions Filed and Data You Can Locate

Divorces In divorce cases, the courts and attorneys usually require detailed financial information on both parties to arrive at a supposedly equitable division of property and to preclude both parties from hiding assets or falsifying their financial worth at the time of divorce. The document dividing property, the *property settlement agreement*, is usually detailed and lists all assets and liabilities at the time of the court filing. This agreement, found in court files, can be invaluable to you, especially because it discloses assets found not only in the county of jurisdiction, but in other counties and states where the parties might have assets. The settlement agreement also often includes other assets that were obtained through inheritance, business dealings, and other means that are not always found or are difficult to find in localized asset searches.

One of the first cases I conducted as a private investigator was to discover a businessman's current activities and financial worth for a divorce case. On the surface, the man had a small but prosperous company and supported his family in an upper-middle-class lifestyle. On my first trip to the county courthouse to search real property records, I was amazed to find that the subject had over forty separate real estate transactions in a partnership with a friend of the client's family.

When the proceeding came to final hearing in the judge's chambers, the opposing attorney filed a financial statement of $360,000 for the husband. Our attorney then placed the husband on the witness stand and questioned him for six hours concerning the other properties. Confronted with the deed records, the husband admitted to assets in excess of $4 million. Without the investigation, the spouse would have agreed to the $360,000 figure, and neither the court nor the client would have known the truth.

Personal Injury Lawsuits Information on lawsuits involving injury claims are extremely important to several kinds of people:

- Employers looking for new employees

- Employers sued in a personal injury case

- Potential insurers

- Persons sued in accidents

Such records will indicate whether a subject has a history of personal injury claims or other types of legal actions pertinent to your problem.

These suit files often contain extensive depositions and detailed descriptions of claimed injuries, as well as financial information relating to the settlement of claims listed in the suits. In my experience, people involved in multiple personal injury lawsuits usually suffer similar injuries and show a pattern of filing insurance claims. Records of personal injury claims are often good sources for asset information on employees you wouldn't normally think were able to build substantial assets.

Financial Claims and Litigation Just as a divorced person knows his or her ex's whereabouts and status at any time, a person who feels beaten out of money and sues for collection often has detailed information on his or her debtor. These creditors often have old financial statements, knowledge of new businesses or assets in other locations, and new addresses on those who have skipped on their debts. Some of these creditors can provide you with the best outside view of an individual's business history or ability to perform on any activities you are interested in learning about.

These suits are often your best source for due diligence or business background information on people or businesses you are examining for acquisitions, mergers, or takeovers. The statements of parties and factual information contained in these lawsuits provide information on how your subject has operated in the past, a key to predicting how he or she will do business in the future. Remember the old saying "A leopard never changes its spots"?

Fraud Claims The last person you want to do business with is someone with a history of fraud. I've found that once a person has committed fraud and gotten away with it, it's easier the next time. Usually, people who commit a fraud develop a pattern and style they tend to repeat, each time aiming higher.

A prudent person should always check fraud cases, particularly when hiring or entering into business relationships with newfound friends. If you even suspect that an employee or business associate is currently defrauding you, it's worth putting that person under the microscope of a civil records search to allay your fears.

Suits in fraud claims are usually well documented, and they outline specifically the fraudulent activities, charges, acts, or omissions alleged against the defendant. Knowing the pattern of someone you suspect can aid you in investigating your current situation. Most people who commit frauds do so repeatedly and, important to you, usually have a pattern. The type of fraud they commit rarely changes, even though the amount they go after may escalate. Knowing how a particular subject has committed a fraud is as important to you as knowing a felon's modus operandi is to the police. This knowledge will also give you clues as to where you should look in your organization or financial operations to detect fraudulent activities.

Court records in fraud claims help you by providing names of witnesses, co-conspirators, and parties who were defrauded. Again, people who believe they were cheated or defrauded have very long memories and are usually most willing to describe their experiences to you. Often they will tell you more than you ever wanted to know about your newfound "friend."

I can hardly imagine any serious record check that doesn't include civil court records. When you check civil records, don't look only for those areas you believe are pertinent to your specific purposes; read everything in the file. Often, you will find the information you need in what may seem to be an unrelated area, and this may well be the key to your case.

Whatever Happened to Johnny? My client was a major retailer in Dallas, and Johnny was one of the company's highest-level executives. The company had recently discovered it was losing money through its vendors, approximately $10 million worth. Because the problem had started in the purchasing department, my client and I suspected that someone in purchasing was the one defrauding the company.

My check of civil court records showed nothing on the clerical personnel but turned up a divorce and child custody action Johnny had taken against his common-law wife, Teresa.

That was odd, I thought, since Teresa's name had not turned up in Johnny's employment application or résumé.

In Johnny's child custody suit, he claimed Teresa had slept with many of his fellow workers, was a prostitute and drug user, and therefore was incapable of caring for their child and that he should be awarded custody.

Obviously, I had to talk to Teresa. It was clear these two people had not parted on friendly terms.

What I found out from Teresa was quite different from Johnny's story in the divorce and custody files. Teresa had lived with Johnny for five years, and during that time his life was one of intrigue and schizophrenia. Over five years, Johnny had assumed four different identities—each used to perpetrate a fraud on a different employer. Johnny considered himself a master of deception and used his prowess to manufacture professional degrees, status and credentials, a solid reputation, and superb educational qualifications from an obscure little university.

Teresa claimed Johnny had bragged to her that he had once met some men on a jet who had known him under a previous identity, but that he lied so convincingly they finally believed him to be the double of the man who had bilked them out of thousands of dollars only months before.

With Teresa's information, I established Johnny's real name and developed additional information that confirmed him as a suspect and perpetrator of the multimillion-dollar fraud.

When confronted with our evidence, Johnny disappeared. He's probably assumed a new identity now and is starting all over, with a new set of credentials and a new employer who has no idea of what lies further down the pike.

BANKRUPTCY: THE NEW GAME IN TOWN

In the not-too-distant past, businesspeople considered bankruptcy the ultimate failure, one of the most shameful events that could occur during their career. Today it's almost as if bankruptcies have become fashionable, a shrewd way to sock away dough and wipe out creditors and debt. If you haven't filed for bankruptcy, you aren't a part of the "in" crowd that wheels, deals, and lives by its wits.

You might think that's an exaggeration, but leaf through the Sunday supplements to your newspaper, check TV ads, scan the yellow pages, and you find scores of lawyers advertising their wizardry at wiping out financial woes and discharging debts. I guarantee you these lawyers wouldn't pay good money to advertise if there weren't a huge market out there looking for ways to skip debts.

Trends to Watch Out For

There are some current trends or "plays" certain professional debtors are trying by using bankruptcy protection, plays so serious that it's important to discuss them here before more general information on bankruptcies. Remember them whenever you want to extend credit to, form business relationships with, or even marry one of the wheeler-dealers in your town.

One trend I've found is that a growing number of people who file for bankruptcy do so with absolutely no intention of completing the action. The debtor using this ploy is counting on creditors' fear of having their claim totally wiped out, coupled with their distaste for the time and expense involved in pursuing their rights in the bankruptcy proceedings. The debtor, in a very sincere-sounding gesture, goes to each creditor and assures him or her individually that the creditor is the one person or company that the debtor wants to see get paid—at least something. So the two enter negotiations and reach a settlement—often at ten to twenty-five cents on the dollar of the claim. Then the debtor goes on to the next creditor and the next, making the same offer.

Once the debtor has settled with all the creditors outside of bankruptcy court, he or she also drops the bankruptcy action. For as little as ten cents on the dollar, the debtor walks away without ever having actually taken a bankruptcy and with a clean bill of financial health.

In another wrinkle of this game, a debtor moves from his or her hometown—Houston, for example—to a distant place like Bangor, Maine, for a short time—six or fewer months—depending on who's watching. While in this distant place, the debtor declares bankruptcy, knowing that creditors often won't make the effort to go out of town or state to follow the bankruptcy proceedings.

Because creditors give up, the debtor ends up having an unopposed bankruptcy proceeding. He or she returns shortly afterward with no debts and no bankruptcy filing back home, the base of his or her operations. This makes it very difficult for local creditors or potential creditors to find a history of bankruptcy.

Because of these trends, it's wise to pursue any defaulting debtors throughout their bankruptcy proceedings and to protect every right you have as a creditor.

The following case I worked on represents everything

that's wrong with the bankruptcy system today and shows how you can be taken advantage of if you don't work hard to protect your rights.

In the mid-1980s, Barry G. put together hundreds of real estate partnerships to buy and sell office buildings and to develop shopping centers. To accomplish this, Barry, acting as the principal, borrowed over $100 million from banks and S&Ls across the country.

In each project, Barry skimmed off loan proceeds, took kickbacks from contractors, and took money advanced by the landlord for renovations that would never be done. He also misapplied the proceeds of construction financing to build himself a $3 million home, complete with an indoor pool and gymnasium. When the projects were completed and the nonexistent tenants he had invented to help convince bankers to make loans didn't move in, Barry couldn't repay the notes that came due.

He went to a prominent bankruptcy legal eagle, who promptly filed a petition claiming Barry had lost all his money in bad business ventures and was unable to pay the $100 million debt.

One creditor, a former business partner of Barry's, knew the bankruptcy was a fraud. Doggedly the partner chased Barry through every bankruptcy hearing and forced him to produce his business records and information on personal assets, exposing at least part of Barry's fraud before the bankruptcy court. However, other creditors, most notably the banks, were either unwilling or not smart enough to follow the former partner's example. They let the bankruptcy run its course through every phase, never challenging Barry's disclosure of his financial position. The court discharged their claims. That bankruptcy, along with others like it, undoubtedly added to the debt that was instrumental in causing the failure of many of our nation's financial institutions.

Where is Barry today? Living well in his $3 million home, waiting out the IRS, and getting ready to develop some new business ventures. The only party who got any money back from Barry's schemes was the former partner who wouldn't let Barry get away.

Where to Find Bankruptcy Records and What They'll Reveal

Bankruptcy is a federal court action. You can find public records on bankruptcy proceedings at the bankruptcy courts in various federal district jurisdictions. These cases are also recorded through private information resellers like Information America and Prentice-Hall Legal and Financial Services.

Here are some important items found in bankruptcy records:

- *Current status of a bankruptcy proceeding*—Completing a bankruptcy action entails several steps such as filing, discovery, motions, hearings, and the like. Each step is important to interested parties in a bankruptcy proceeding, and the court has specific rules for answers and proceedings so parties can maintain their rights and claims.

- *Creditors' list*—This list provides the names, addresses, and amounts of money owed to creditors of the bankrupt party.

- *List of the subject's debts and assets at the time of bank-ruptcy*—If the filer petitioning for bankruptcy doesn't list all his or her debtors, then the court cannot discharge the debt. However, more important to you as you search the records—especially if you happen to be one of the creditors on the creditors' list—is the subject's list of assets. As Barry G.'s former partner found out, the statement of the professional debtor is unlikely to reveal all his or her assets. If you find yourself in a position similar to that of the former partner (you have good reason to believe all the subject's assets are not listed), then you must contest the subject's representations and fight for your rights and fair share at every step of the proceeding.

Why Bankruptcy Records Are Important

Most of the uses for bankruptcy records are pretty obvious. Still, here's a list for your reference:

- *To track a person's bankruptcy proceedings*—If you don't do this carefully, you stand a good chance of losing your claims as uncontested, thus missing opportunities to find out the true nature of your subject's reasons for filing.

- *To determine someone's business record and back-ground*—Bankruptcy records can give you insight into what caused a person to fail. Sure, it could have been bad luck or general business climate. On the other hand, the failure could have been part of some grand scheme, and this is a good place to start putting that puzzle together.

- *To examine an individual's character*—How a subject behaves in a bankruptcy can show you how the subject treats his or her other obligations and responsibilities.

- *To uncover assets or reveal how a person hides them*—When combined and compared with other records and sources of information, bankruptcy records can be invaluable in a general asset search or in discovering whether a subject has perpetrated a fraud. Bankruptcy court usually requires extensive discovery, which can be invaluable to anyone trying to make a claim on assets or piece together a person's financial condition and method of doing business.

4

WHAT'S IT WORTH?

When someone comes to you with a business deal, how do you know what it's worth? Do you take the word of the potentially glib-tongued developer and trust his or her projections of a five-to-one return on your money? If there is one thing you should remember in doing business with anyone, it's that if it sounds too good to be true, it probably is.

Tommy Runyon offered owners of vacant buildings a deal they couldn't refuse. He promised to renovate their empty shopping centers into multiscreen theater complexes and turn their vacant strip centers into "cash cows." For only a small cash advance sufficient to put in theater seats, a sound system, and projection equipment (usually for about $1 million), Tommy promised to turn the vacant properties into city focal points that would provide jobs, cash flow, and neighborhood centers any community could be proud of.

What Tommy never told property owners and financiers was that his wife owned the corporation that did the decorating and renovation and that the theaters were not, as promised, being stocked with new, state-of-the-art equipment but with used theater seats and sound systems torn out of the other theaters Tommy had skipped out on in other cities.

The FBI and the leaders of several municipalities are still looking for Tommy, who has left in his wake more than a $200 million debt and a new group of failed financial institutions that once helped cities finance programs to improve their communities.

What might it have been worth for these property owners, bankers, and city leaders to have briefly searched the records before attempting to do business with good ol' Tommy? At least $200 million!

REAL ESTATE RECORDS

Once someone becomes the owner of a home or other real estate, that person most assuredly becomes a fixture in the community and the county grantee/grantor records through various mortgages, easements, deeds, and other legal documents.

The Importance of Real Estate Records

Because the home and other real estate of someone you are investigating are usually that person's most significant assets, real property records are extremely valuable in determining your subject's net worth. Here are some ways you can use real estate records:

- To verify independently the claimed assets of a subject

- To help determine the indebtedness of your subject and current encumbrances against his or her property

- To determine additional assets unclaimed or hidden by someone

- To locate people who knew the subject's activities or whereabouts before or after the sale of property

- To ascertain whether the subject has a mortgage from which you can determine the subject's payment history

- To locate trustees and nominees (straw men)

What You'll Find in Real Estate Records

Each real estate purchase is documented by a general or special warranty deed or, in some cases, by a contract for sale that documents the purchase of properties or buildings.

If the property is financed, the person receiving the financing will grant a deed of trust to the mortgage institution in order to secure the mortgage and list the dollar amount of the debt to the lender.

In addition to a correct legal description of the property, including easements, these documents usually will indicate in some way the value of the property, either through the tax assessment on the warranty deed or the amount of the mortgage and down payment. The mortgage company is usually named as the party holding a lien on the property. The title company also will be named somewhere in the documents. Remember that the mortgage company may not currently be servicing the note; lenders often sell loans to other institutions. If you are trying to discover how a mortgagee is performing on a debt, you will have to get the current note holder's name from the original lender specified on the documents.

Further, every activity that takes place in the county concerning the property is a matter of public record filed against the legal description of a property. Thus, by looking up the records associated with a given legal description, you can learn about easements to lay utilities or cable TV lines, notices to taxpayers, filings of or on deed restrictions, and other activities.

Finally, you now have a way to help find those who know about a subject before or after a purchase or sale— either the previous or the new owners listed in the property file. Most real estate transactions are more of a process than an event, with some documents and verification still needed after the sale. Often the people who sold the property know where the subject came from before purchasing their property. Likewise, people who buy from your subject usually know where that person went and probably have an idea what he or she is doing—information that is good to have if you want to locate the subject or are trying to find unexplained gaps in his or her activities.

Suggestions for Using Real Estate Records

Real estate, property sales, and the documents used to record the transfer of real estate can be complex. Here are two pointers that might help you use what could be valuable records.

Study the Process If you don't have a good handle on the process, take a little time to study it. Familiarize yourself with the various common transactions and documents, and learn the functions of the documents as they relate to property transfer. Even then, realize that few people can understand every complex document available for all the different types of sales and transfers in addition to the various partnerships and other legal entities that make up complicated transactions.

Don't be afraid to seek expert help if you get in over your head; go to a real estate agent, a real property researcher, or title company examiner. I'm not suggesting you should shy away from doing this work yourself, because most of the records are easily accessible and easy to understand. But some transactions can be messy and hard to follow; don't let the difficult ones stop you. In fact, these may be the most important ones to unravel and check out, because often they were intentionally designed to be obscure.

Examine Documents as Well as Records Make sure you examine not only the real property indexes to determine the type of real estate transactions conducted by the subject, but also the actual deeds and transfer documents themselves. Study *all* the deeds and transfer documents, and often you will find the needed breadth of information, such as the purchaser's main mortgage lender and the amount loaned, as well as the appraised property value.

By combining these points when you evaluate real estate records, you will get the most out of your search. Then you can use those records for far more than you might have anticipated. Consider the following story of what searching real estate records can do for you.

Jimmy Bell, a former postal worker, left Houston,

skipping out on his wife, his children, and his debts, destroying all personal records of his employment and personal history he could get his hands on. For some reason, he was trying to disappear completely and was doing a pretty good job of it, because everywhere I looked was a dead end.

But Jimmy missed a crucial item. He sold his house. By itself, that posed no problem for him; it was a quick, down-and-dirty sale. But what Jimmy didn't know, that I did, was that title companies usually retain some money after the sale in an escrow account, usually about $1,000, which is used to pay extra expenses. The money stays in escrow for thirty to sixty days until the company is sure there aren't any problems undisclosed at the time of sale. These are problems the seller had warranted against, such as an unsound building foundation, termite problems, and the like. The escrowed funds are sent to the seller once the escrow period has elapsed.

By going to the title company that closed the sale and obtaining a copy of the front and back of the escrow check, I found through the bank codes stamped on his deposit that the check had been cashed in Hot Springs, Arkansas. Once I found his new town, locating Jimmy through utility records was a cinch.

Imagine Jimmy's surprise when our investigators showed up at his door to serve him with a contempt of court citation for nonpayment of child support and an order for him to appear in court on that day. I understand that Jimmy made a quick settlement with his wife, then disappeared again. What was he really running from? I don't know, but I'll bet I could find him again if I wanted to.

TAX RECORDS

Every city and county, some states, and many other taxing authorities such as school districts tax real or tangible property as a major source of revenue. This property includes real estate; business assets such as inventory, furniture, and equipment; and personal assets such as boats, airplanes, and automobiles. Exactly what is taxed and what is exempted differs according to the need or greed of your jurisdiction.

Some states have consolidated local property tax assessing and appraisal functions, which allows unified taxation throughout any one district and usually corresponds to county boundaries. These states have done so for two reasons: (1) to reduce the numbers of people performing the same functions in overlapping taxing jurisdictions, and (2) because of attempts to truly perform ad valorem, or true-market-value property appraisals. Before consolidation, a city and county may have established different valuations for the same properties. Consolidation ends that, making it easier for you to check tax assessor records.

What Tax Assessor Records Reveal

From tax assessor records, you can obtain a few potentially important pieces of information.

A Complete Legal Description On real estate, the complete legal description of the property includes dimensions; plat, lot, and street number; county survey information, including development and dates transferred; and any improvements to the property such as the construction of additional houses, buildings, or pools. Identifying a subject's real property is, of course, important to you as an investigator trying to find outside information on the true financial status of your target. But remember, once you have identified real property through tax records, you still must document it properly through real property records at the county.

Current Assessed Valuation States recently have made concerted efforts to make truer ad valorem assessments on real estate at its "highest and best use," so you'll find current tax assessor appraisals are pretty close to the true current market value of property. However, large errors or significant and legitimate differences of opinion between property owners and valuation authorities often arise from at least four major problems faced by taxing authorities in making accurate assessment valuations:

1. Valuing agricultural land that is near or contiguous to an urban area

2. Valuing undeveloped property in an urban area, especially in a center of rapid development

3. Valuing agricultural land known to have undeveloped but marketable mineral resources

4. Valuing improvements, especially new construction, in an urban area suffering severe recession and rapidly declining property values

Taxpayer's Current Status Tax assessor records indicate whether a property owner is current on his or her taxes and how much the owner owes and has paid in the last few years. The appraisal data thus help you establish the true current financial condition of an individual. Considering that people generally will let other bills slide before they get behind on their taxes, if a person is delinquent on a large tax bill, chances are that person is already in deep trouble.

Clues About Net Worth Assessor records also provide independent verification of a subject's net worth. You can't really consider a tax assessor the ultimate source for determining whether your subject's position is as he or she claimed. But the assessor's data can be a good initial step toward piecing together complex puzzles such as the search for assets of companies or people who have extensive property holdings in different locations.

A Tip to Remember Keep in mind that the taxpayer is not always the property owner. In some of the more important large-dollar criminal cases, such as the investigations of Manuel Noriega, knowing this fact has proved particularly valuable to people trying to determine a suspect's assets and financial activity.

Properties identified as belonging to Manuel Noriega have shown up in other men's names on legal title and tax records. Many appear to be in the name of a former Spaniard turned Panamanian. He is reputed to be Noriega's real estate buyer in transactions totaling over $200 million throughout the world.

How did we get this information? I just happened to be in Panama during the 1989 invasion, sitting in a bar when parachutes blossomed all over the sky. Our investigators watched from the rooftop bar as Marines cleared the streets and chased a squad of soldiers out of the house of Carlos Whitgreen, Noriega's finance minister. Seeing a unique opportunity, we ran into the burning house and bagged every document, paper, and computer disk we could find, then hightailed it back to the bar. Among the items we nabbed were a computer listing of the properties, bank accounts, and names that Noriega hid money in all over the world.

How did we happen to be in the right place at the right time? Just lucky, I guess.

UTILITY RECORDS

One of the first services humans developed to make life more pleasant was a reliable water supply and some kind of refuse removal or sewer system. Eventually, no home was complete without clean running water and a waste removal system.

Most modern public utility companies are owned by nonprofit corporations or municipalities, which maintain their customer names and addresses in computer databases so that they can be easily serviced and billed. Fortunately for you, those records are, for the most part, readily available to investigators.

Generally, a phone call to your public utility will get you the name of the person who is billed at the address you give. The utility representative will also tell you if a particular person lives within the service area and usually will give you the address without much of a hassle. If the person you are speaking with seems reluctant, a little sweet talk will usually persuade him or her to give you the data.

That's what happened when Intertect, Inc., was hired by an insurance company to track down Freddy Fontenot. The insurers believed that all the furniture and valuables Freddy claimed were destroyed in a recent fire at his home might, if we were lucky, be found at Freddy's new address.

Jane, the investigator we assigned, called the electric company and verified a new utility listing for good ol' Freddy in a little town about thirty miles south of Houston. The service had been hooked up a week before Freddy's sad event, suggesting he had miraculously anticipated the tragedy and just might have "shifted" a few precious items beforehand.

Taking advantage of the timely arrival of New Year's Eve, Jane and Julie, another of our investigators, knocked on Freddy's door at 10:00 P.M., each appearing slightly tipsy, dressed provocatively, and "ready to party." They told the hapless impromptu host they had lost their way to another party. After a single lingering stare, Freddy couldn't wait to invite the two ladies into his new home so that he could convince them a party was about to begin right there.

While Jane stopped in Freddy's living room to use the phone, Julie asked to use the powder room. Her eager host led her through the house to the bathroom.

In a few minutes, Jane and Julie identified three unique items Freddy had claimed were destroyed in the fire. Their charade gave them enough information to convince themselves (and a judge in court the next morning) that Freddy's fire was premeditated and his claim was fraudulent.

Jane still chuckles whenever she recalls Freddy's expression as she took the witness stand and described the items he had just tearfully claimed had burned. The jurors noticed his look, too, and rained all over Freddy's insurance claim parade. Little does he know that his own arrogance and stupidity in leaving a clear trail in utility records would wipe out his best-laid plans.

WILLS AND PROBATE

Probate records include wills and inheritance history that show the dispersal of assets and liabilities after someone's death. When it comes to determining an individual's net worth or discovering his or her assets, they are among the most unknown, unused, and overlooked documents. Unfortunately, most investigators just don't think to look for wealth through inheritance.

In one of the largest Texas insurance fraud cases, one that seriously depleted the state board's resources, the state completely overlooked valuable land inherited by one of the principals of the company involved in the case. Finally, in a deposition, a secretary related her discussion with an officer of the company about a required listing of assets. From her deposition, we discovered this principal had decided not to list some significant inherited property in the Southeast because "They don't need to know that, do they?" This inheritance information was crucial and condemning, and it was not long before the state's investigators closed their case against the principal.

Record checks are a process, not just a simple review of selected individual documents. Probate records are a classic example. In this case, the process includes thinking about who your subject could have inherited property from.

The most likely sources of an inheritance are a person's parents or grandparents. Thus, at a minimum, you'll want to know the names and locations of your subject's parents and grandparents. Where can you find this information?

First, remember that parents' names and addresses are

among the pieces of information on a marriage license. Thus, when you check marriage licenses, you should collect this information for possible use in a probate check. You also might try using your target's Social Security number to locate his or her parents' home county, as described in Chapter 1.

Even more important, in all cases and issues involving large sums of money, lawyers should ask witnesses and subjects the names and addresses of parents and grandparents, living or dead.

Investigators also should request the subject's parents' names and addresses, and inquire about favored relatives or relatives who might bless the subject with an inheritance.

Frequently, attorneys and investigators are so wrapped up in the complexities of a case they fail to ask some simple questions. Whatever you do, in large money cases and settlement issues, always ask for parents' names and addresses, or make sure you find out where they live. Here's what can happen if you don't:

Edwin Ball milked his S&L, commonly called Gangland Savings, for a huge salary and a number of allegedly fraudulent dealings with insiders. The Federal Savings and Loan Insurance Corporation (FSLIC) and Federal Home Loan Bank Board (FHLBB) had just closed Ball's S&L after the institution had taken $100 million in questionable losses. After examining Ball to determine whether or not he could be a potential defendant for damages, the FSLIC sued him personally to recover the millions of dollars that began the events leading to the S&L's failure.

The regulators hired a prominent law firm to examine Ball's assets, and the firm quickly ran up a bill of over

$100,000. The attorneys, paralegals, and "investigators" finally concluded that the former president didn't have enough assets even to pay for the cost of the litigation, should the regulators decide to pursue him, much less to make restitution for any damages.

The problem was that this law firm didn't search county probate records, which would have told the lawyers that Edwin Ball had inherited over $16 million at 1960 values. He had inherited real estate, oil and gas interests, cash, bonds, insurance proceeds, and a West Texas ranch that at today's values could have amounted to over $50 million. Those assets were still in Ball's name, a matter of public record, and not only would have paid for the litigation, but also reduced the government's debt incurred through the institution's failure.

Unfortunately, the regulators and their expensive law firm dropped the ball, and the banker laughed all the way to his luxurious home. The statute of limitations expired, and he couldn't be prosecuted for what was one of the largest S&L failures in Texas.

In probate matters, the court appoints an executor to conduct an investigation that will determine the assets and liabilities of the person's estate. The executor then supervises the dispersal of assets according to the deceased's will. He or she is responsible for distributing assets and clearing liabilities. Many states require executors to be bonded to protect the creditors of estates. In cases where the deceased died intestate (without a will), the court disposes of assets and liabilities according to state law.

By examining assets and liabilities left in an estate, you can determine a deceased's financial position at death. The records will also list the name and addresses of heirs and give some indication of the value of the cash, insurance policies, bank accounts, and other property willed to the lucky heirs.

When you're looking for assets, the older your target is, the likelier it is that he or she might have inherited some assets or proceeds from an insurance policy from parents or some other family member. Many people originally acquired their wealth through inheritance from a family member, and that family member might have lived far from the subject's home or locale. Therefore, you may have to do some digging to find the information you need.

MISCELLANEOUS PERSONAL RECORDS: THE "JUNK FILES"

Most government and legal jurisdictions—state, county, and city—keep what amounts to a junk file, a hodgepodge of records that don't fit into any specific department. Exactly what goes into these miscellaneous personal records (MPRs) varies from jurisdiction to jurisdiction, but it is always interesting and informative.

What's in MPRs and Where to Find Them

It's almost impossible to give a laundry list of the types of records that can be kept in MPRs. But here is one good rule of thumb: *anyone required by the state or local government to be registered to work to do business will have a record attesting to that fact.* A wide variety of professions and jobs must be registered, including nurses, doctors, real estate agents, lawyers, dentists, beauticians and barbers, some contractors, chemical handlers, notaries, and many others.

In some cases, these registrations will be recorded in an appropriate department, especially on the state level, but they might also be found on the county level in MPRs, especially if the work or function requires some sort of surety, performance, or notary bond. Usually, the first place to look for MPRs is at the county courthouse.

MPRs on the county level used to include, and in some cases still do, military discharge forms, or DD-214s. These forms give you a veteran's complete military history, including discharge, domestic and foreign service, awards, and any disciplinary charges.

Some Benefits and Uses of MPRs

So many types of records and registrations are kept in MPRs, and their locations are so varied, that it's difficult to anticipate what your needs are in checking them out. However, here are some general thoughts on how they might help you. To guide your search, be creative and apply what you know about what is found in MPRs.

Making Sure a Person Is Bonded Anyone can say he or she has gone through proper bonding procedures. Actually obtaining a required bond is another thing. A fraudulent bond isn't worth the paper it's printed on.

Helping to Locate Missing Persons A person might try to hide out, but someone who wants to practice a licensed trade might still be registered with his or her professional licensing authority or association. That registration might include an accurate current address.

Locating Notary Publics I could almost write an entire chapter on locating notary publics, especially if I wanted to write a book of case histories. In many legal disputes, lawyers (or anyone for that matter) need to find people who witnessed legal documents to attest to the truth and completeness of notarized documents, especially documents being used as evidence, if the validity of those documents is in question. By finding the legal secretary or whoever acted as notary, you might be able to find information that casts doubt on the document's integrity.

The subject of notaries, notary bonds, and secretaries should be compelling. Secretaries don't have to be registered, but notaries do, and often a business's secretary and notary are the same person. Why is that important? Because like ex-spouses and ex-partners, this person may know more (often even more than an ex-spouse) about the boss than anyone else. What's more, what secretaries know is sometimes more valuable to you than an ex-spouse's information. If this secretary who is a notary happens to be an "ex-secretary," then you may really have something.

That was true of Joyce, who had been Jerry's secretary, confidante, and general all-around life planner for ten years. When Jerry's business ran into trouble during a downturn in the mid-1980s, he began selling off assets and dispersing records and business accounts to other, newly formed corporations he set up. Then he attempted to sell his building back to the insurance company by torching it. Overnight, his net worth rose through a $10 million claim, an insurance policy that he was treating like a CD.

The insurance company filed a civil suit claiming that the fire was caused by the insured, Jerry.

Motive isn't required to prove a criminal case of arson in court, though it does help criminal investigators make their case by pointing them in the right direction to look for hard evidence. However, motive is essential to civil cases of arson, especially when an insurance company is contesting a claim. Often, motive can cast doubts on an insured's claim and can reduce the claim if the doubt is conveyed strongly enough.

At first, criminal investigators didn't have enough hard evidence to indict Jerry, and they had not yet determined a motive. Our problem was to put together the pieces of the puzzle on the corporate transfers, coupled with company losses, to prove an economic motive and financial gain from the fire.

Investigators discovered Jerry had dismissed his secretary a week before the fire, which I thought was odd, considering her long history with him. The trouble was, we couldn't locate Joyce. She had moved to another part of town and had an unlisted telephone number.

Rather than searching all the other routes, I started by checking records of notary public filings. There was Joyce, waiting to be found, working for another firm and still a notary. The notary records gave her Social Security number, her current employer, her new home address, and the name of her current bondholder.

It turned out Joyce had asked Jerry too many questions about his new expensive lifestyle. I don't know whether he fired Joyce to protect her or because she was too nosy—maybe he just wanted to keep all the money for himself. I do know Joyce was madder than hell at being fired and was willing to discuss Jerry's financial activities in detail. Her comments provided the information we needed to keep the insurance company from paying Jerry's claim and gave the prosecutor grounds to reopen a criminal investigation.

MILITARY SERVICE RECORDS

First off, there's no truth to the commonly held belief that military service records are confidential. The truth is, many military records are a matter of public record. With good cause, anyone can make a Freedom of Information Act (FOIA) request to obtain military records.

Have you ever tried to find an old friend in the military? Maybe, a soldier proposed to you and then disappeared on maneuvers. Contact the Defense Locater Service or military locater services of the forces branches in Washington, D.C. With a subject's Social Security number, the locater services can tell you whether the soldier is still on active duty and where he or she is stationed, or if the person was terminated and discharged.

You can also attempt to locate a soldier at a base where you believe he or she is stationed or might have been stationed. If, when you request information, someone at the base tells you that he or she can't give you the information, then you're talking to the wrong person. Ask for the Freedom of Information Act officer, who is usually in the public affairs office. This officer will know the law and will give you the information legally available, as well as the procedures that will help you locate your subject.

There are books available that specialize in locating and identifying military personnel. You can get valuable information and help from a number of books published in recent years that identify personnel in the military by service and rank (officers, noncommissioned officers, warrant officers, etc.). Another valuable book, *How to Locate Anyone Who Has Been in the Military*, guides you through the swamp of military record sources and helps you locate anyone who has been in or is currently in the armed forces.

Finally, don't forget that you can use county records for the DD-214s found in the MPR files, especially for those who served before 1976. While you're at it, search the county's full records in the town where your subject was discharged. If he or she was there for a while, your subject probably had a loan filed in UCCs, a divorce, or a voter registration.

GOVERNMENT DATA ON THE TRANSPORTATION INDUSTRY

Other sources of information include the Federal Aviation Administration (FAA) and the National Transportation Safety Board (NTSB). Contacting these federal agencies may seem a bit farfetched, but whenever you're checking someone out or trying to locate someone, you need to use whatever resources are available.

FAA Data

There are many ways to locate or find out about someone who happens to be a pilot. But if you know your subject is a pilot, often the best way to find out about him or her is to search through the records of the Federation Aviation Administration. Located in Oklahoma City, the FAA can provide a world of information about pilots or aircraft:

- *Whether a subject has been or is currently a licensed pilot*—This record includes various types of identifying

information, such as address, date of birth, flying qualifications, Social Security number, and physical description.

- *Physical examination information*—Once a year, the
FAA requires licensed pilots to take and pass a physical
examination. That information is kept on file with the
pilot's license. The record will show where the last physical was taken and whether the physical and certification
are up for renewal in the next month or two.

- *Detailed records on aircraft*—The FAA also keeps detailed information about each plane, filed according to
the aircraft's ±N′ number registration. The data include
last known location and owner of the aircraft, number of
hours flown, and history of scheduled maintenance. This
information is most helpful when locating or identifying
aircraft.

- *Accident investigation information*—All material on
plane crashes and accidents becomes a matter of public
record once the FAA's investigation is complete. The
FAA's compiled information on crashes, accidents, and
their causes is quite comprehensive and can save your
lawyer much time and money in an aircraft accident
case.

Earlier I said you should remember to use all the
resources at your disposal. The following story illustrates
why you should.

Many years ago—fourteen to be exact—my firm had
been trying to serve Bill Payne with a witness subpoena,
and he had successfully avoided it for months. Then we

found out he was a pilot, and we discovered from the FAA that Bill was scheduled for a recertification physical in two weeks. With this information in our bag, our investigators waited for Bill at the doctor's office (the FAA has regionally approved doctors for flight physicals) and successfully served him with the papers. Easy as can be.

NTSB Data

The National Transportation Safety Board is primarily concerned with information about safety and accidents on commercial carriers—aircraft, rail, and other forms of commercial transport such as buses. The agency conducts exhaustive investigations of accidents, especially those that cause significant injuries or deaths. The NTSB is also a good source of compiled and detailed site, type, and general accident information.

Like data on FAA investigations, NTSB data become public once the investigation is completed, and can be ordered for a small fee. If a friend or loved one is killed or injured in a transportation accident, you can do no greater service than to help his or her surviving relatives get this information. It may save them a great deal of investigative fees and help them understand what really happened.

PROFESSIONAL ASSOCIATIONS AND LICENSING BOARDS

Almost every occupation that passes itself off as a profession has a regulatory and licensing board that sets guidelines and charges dues to the industry and its practitioners. Most occupations and even many avocations have associations as well.

You'll find most professional boards and associations in your state's capital. For national associations, check first in Washington, D.C., or its environs, such as Arlington, Falls Church, or Alexandria, Virginia, or neighboring cities in Maryland. If you intend to do any records checks, get hold of your city, state capital, and the Washington, D.C., phone books for ready reference. If you can't find a state or national association in or around the capitals, then call someone in the industry in your city, and ask that person where the headquarters of his or her industry association is located.

Generally, associations and boards can provide a wealth of knowledge and insight into their trade and its practitioners. Here are some kinds of information to look for:

- Industry guidelines and standards, general information on industry or association membership
- Licensing information on specific members, along with areas of recognized specialization
- Current business addresses of members
- Any history of business complaints, grievances, or charges against members

Since many of the associations act as self-regulating bodies, you might also find out whether or not the board or association has run any investigations on your subject. While this information may not be easy to get, you might still find out the outcome of the investigation, if not all of the specifics. If you are involved in a lawsuit, you can ask your lawyer to subpoena the rest.

Some Reasons for Checking Association and Board Records

One of our standard reasons for checking is to corroborate industry or professional credentials and affiliations. However, don't overlook this critical point: if you *suspect* your subject is passing himself or herself off with phony degrees or credentials, check out that person. Almost all professionals have some sort of professional affiliation, and this information is just too easy to find out to ignore.

Profession Peeking

Consider whether your subject is licensed, registered, certified, or given a diploma announcing his or her expertise to the world. Here are a few suggestions for finding people through their professional affiliations:

- *Accountants*—Check with the American Institute of Certified Public Accountants (AICPA), headquartered in New York City. Each state and many cities also have chapters. Any of them can quickly tell you whether your subject is a member.

- *Attorneys*—The national organization is the American Bar Association (ABA), in Chicago. Additionally, each state has a bar association. Each state bar has a licensing procedure and maintains membership in local and county associations.

- *Bankers*—Contact the American Bankers Association (ABA), in New York City. Also, state banking commissions register bank officers and directors in the state.

- *Captains of motor vessels and boats*—Contact the U.S. Coast Guard in Washington, D.C., or the marine inspection office in your area.

- *Doctors*—Many belong to the American Medical Association (AMA), which has headquarters in Chicago. Doctors are also licensed by each state, most often in the state capital.

- *Electricians, plumbers, and contractors*—Besides looking up city permits, don't forget to check with unions and professional associations. Check in the library or your phone book for telephone numbers and addresses.

- *Engineers*—Engineers are licensed by most states and may have several national affiliations, depending on specializations such as civil, electrical, structural, or chemical engineering.

- *Nurses*—Registered Nurses (RNs), and Licensed Vocational Nurses (LVNs) are registered and licensed by each state and are often members of several professional nursing associations. The state board can usually give you the current license/work addresses of nurses registered in its state.

- *Police*—Even local police officers are certified by their state. Their entire file—including education, charges, grievances, and current employment—is a matter of public record.

- *Fire fighters*—Like police officers, fire fighters are registered and certified by a state association. State records will verify education, certification, and specific training, as well as membership, grievances, and problems.

- *Private investigators*—Most states license private investigators. Their full files are a matter of public record for you to explore before ever hiring one.

- *Insurance agents and brokers*—Insurance agents and brokers are licensed and registered by each state through a state insurance board. Records will verify an agent or broker's address and the companies he or she is authorized to write insurance through. That information may lead you to documentation of your subject's sources of income, residuals, and commissions.

- *Bail bondsmen*—Bondsmen are usually licensed in each state under a board. You'll also find them in the yellow pages.

- *Real estate agents*—Salespeople and brokers are registered in each state, either individually or through the company holding their real estate licenses. Most states also have real estate associations that attempt strong self-regulation of their industry. Most people involved in real estate are members of these associations. Additionally, those affiliated with large chains such as Red Carpet and Century 21 are also in national databases and can be located by calling company headquarters.

- *Security guards*—Look under your state board of private investigators/security officers to locate a guard who witnessed an accident or wrote a report you desperately need.

- *Stockbrokers, bond salespeople, traders, and investment bankers*—The National Association of Securities Dealers (NASD), located in New York City, and the Securities and Exchange Commission (SEC) in Washington, D.C., regulate the sale of securities such as stocks and bonds. The NASD is a self-governing association but is very powerful. It registers and licenses brokers, salespeople, traders, and principals, as well as investment firms. The SEC is a government agency that maintains files on grievances, charges, and investigations. Each state also has its own registration procedure through a state securities board and can give you information on the location and status of securities dealers.

- *Teachers*—Teachers are licensed and certified in every state, and most often they are registered through state and national teaching associations such as the National Education Association, Washington, D.C. Teachers may also belong to national and state associations devoted to their specialties such as music, science, math, or vocational or special education.

- *Travel agents*—The Airline Reporting Corporation (ARC) in Washington, D.C., registers agents and agencies writing tickets on all major airlines. So does the American Society of Travel Agents (ASTA), based in New York City.

5

ON-LINE ACCESSIBILITY

ON-LINE COMPUTER AND INFORMATION SERVICES

Before embarking on a records search in the old days, you needed to dose up on antihistamines in order to protect yourself from all the dust that flew when you cracked open those old red books in county clerks' offices. The search process was dull and laborious, consuming hours for even the simplest task. Besides, records searches require so many person-hours that often they were just too expensive.

However, in the 1960s, I discovered that some counties had begun to put voter registrations and tax records on microfiche. Then some states began to contract out their listings of driver's license records, motor vehicle registrations, and property transactions to private resellers like Redi-Data Services, Information America, and Prentice-

Hall Legal and Financial Services. I realized that through widespread accessibility, public records had truly become public.

When I opened my own firm in 1974, I began to build an investigative library of microfilm, microfiche, and directories. As computer access became even more available, I incorporated that into my work, too. Our own files and on-line sources allowed Intertect to run faster, more effective, and less costly checks of records. Soon we could run our checks so quickly and inexpensively that even women who just wanted to check out their dates could afford our services.

Computer access to many files, especially on a large scale, is a reasonable and most likely the wisest course for you to pursue. This investigation technique is so easy and there is so much help to access so much information on nearly everyone, that if you fail to take advantage of it, you could be missing an easy solution to your research problem. Through on-line information from county and state records, information brokers, information resellers, gateways, and major databases—all described in this chapter— you can quickly retrieve information on any subject from voter registrations to blood types to business activities for the past decade.

How to Access Computer Files

To access computerized records, start by calling your county clerk and court clerks to find out what records they have on microfiche or which records they provide computer access to. Each metropolitan area or county is progressing at a different pace in computerizing information and making it easier to access. The larger counties and cities, especially in the western states, were among the first to provide computer access. Before long, most jurisdictions will have computer records or some other form of easy access through an information gateway such as Information America and Prentice-Hall Legal and Financial Services.

Next, determine just how much record checking you want to do, what records you need to focus on, and the locales of your concentration. Essentially, you have several options, and you should be prepared to use any or all separately or in combination, remembering that you might still need to spend some time actually examining the documents themselves to see the whole story.

If you intend to go professional and become either a private investigator or information broker, you can purchase documents or access public records directly from the county or state. These might include microfiche records of voter registrations or computer access to court records, real estate files, and so on.

If you use this service only occasionally, your most economical source is an *information reseller*. Companies such as Prentice-Hall Legal and Financial Services or Information America gather and sell public records information for a fee. Often, these companies can get records from jurisdictions, especially in major metropolitan areas, that aren't yet making their records readily available to the public.

You can also contact *gateway companies* that are subscribers to data sources. These companies resell access to other companies on a per-use basis.

Likelier, you will find your best sources for occasional records searches are information brokers and professional on-line investigators. When deciding which source you will use, the two main factors you should consider are cost and coverage.

Major Sources of General Information

Many vendors offer a variety of services, with more cropping up all the time. In fact, there are so many that sometimes the sheer number of choices is the sole reason for using information brokers or gateways, at least when you start searching public records.

The best way to learn how to use these services is to join one of them (most subscription fees are minimal or nonexistent) and to take the training offered by the suppliers. Additionally, you can subscribe to a number of PC magazines such as *On Line Access* and *PC Computing*, which can be found at many newsstands.

The key to using these services is knowing how to properly search for the information you require and to confine your search to the narrowest limits that meet its requirements. This minimizes your expense and time used in searching these sources.

The following paragraphs describe a number of the databases and information sources that we use and that I've found to be the most helpful in investigations.

Dialog Through Dialog, you can access over 560 database systems with information on individuals' and companies' backgrounds, employment histories, professional papers, and technical information. The services we use most are the Marquis Who's Who, Medline, Standard and Poor's, and Professional Employment databases. To get the most from this source, request the Dialog brochure, and go to one of the company's classes.

CompuServe A Database similar to Dialog, CompuServe offers electronic news, business, personal, and financial information databases. This source is geared more toward personal information than business. It includes many other computer-related services such as electronic bulletin boards.

Prentice-Hall Legal and Financial Services Prentice-Hall Legal and Financial Services, a division of Simon & Schuster, provides a wide range of on-line computer services to attorneys, financial institutions, insurance companies, credit reporters, private investigators, and the federal government. It provides court records information in twenty-four or more states and is rapidly expanding into most if not all states in the near future, providing public records information to your computer terminal. Available records include bankruptcy filings, real estate information, state and federal tax liens, judgments, Uniform Commercial Code filings, corporation and limited partnership information, and corporate charter data.

Through a new venture, Prentice-Hall Online, this company is establishing offices in court records centers around the country to assist its clients in obtaining copies of actual court documents and filings. Also available is a service that provides customized research into many types of pubic records filings.

If you require raw data rather than an investigative research analysis, this type of service will satisfy many of your needs.

Redi-Data Services On the databases from Redi-Data, you can look up information from tax assessors and on grantor/grantee indexes in many major cities throughout the United States. As far as I know, Redi-Data is the most cost-effective means of getting real estate information on a national basis.

Periodical and Professional Paper Databases

Almost all major newspapers and most magazines, trade journals, and even scientific and professional papers are in some database these days. These are all great sources for public information with which you can supplement your records checks. They can even be invaluable in showing you where to look. For example, a story about a business executive involved in a major lawsuit can send you to the correct court to find information on witnesses, proceedings, and the ultimate disposition of a case.

Services that provide newspaper, magazine, and professional paper databases can provide a history of articles published concerning individuals and businesses in their coverage area faster than you can read the copy.

Here are some major on-line sources for periodicals and professional papers:

- *VU/TEXT Information Services, Inc.*, is a database with various news information items. Particularly useful is its on-line services to various publications for locating articles on individuals or businesses throughout the United States in newspapers, magazines, and professional papers.

- *DataTimes* is another newspaper database that is expanding internationally.

- *Magazine Index* is a database of over 370 major American and Canadian magazines dating back to 1959. Access is through Dialog.

- *United Press International* is an around-the-clock news service. It mainly offers raw news but also has stock market information, special business reports, and sports information. You can access it through THE SOURCE or Dialog.

- *Newsearch* is a database that includes 400 magazines, 700 law journals and newspapers, 1,500 trade journals, and 5 major newspapers. It is updated daily and contains files that go back about ten years. Access is through Dialog.

- *Nexis* is a database of eleven major newspapers, fifty magazines, dozens of newsletters, and files on specific data such as business, finance, government, and technology. To access, use Mead Data Central.

- *Newsnet* is another database that contains major newspapers, government publications, magazines, and newsletters. Newsnet information is broken down by sources and subjects. The topics include advertising and marketing, automotive, construction, chemical, communications, accounting, finance, energy, health, insurance, law, public relations, manufacturing, publishing, real estate, social sciences, and many more. Access is through Newsnet.

These are by no means all the available databases on published material. More are coming on-line all the time.

This list shows that there is a vast amount of material available from which to build background information (especially if you use services that store data on professional papers). Note that major vendors contain or access multiples of databases—so many, in fact, that they are sometimes difficult to keep up with. In using them, you are limited only by your own creativity and the potential cost.

If you don't have a computer or don't want to incur the on-line costs, you can find many of the periodicals and newspapers stored at your local library. Almost every library has a reference room and alphabetical index that will help you find articles about the people and information you are seeking. A growing number of libraries now have their own access to the on-line databases described in this chapter and can help you by providing a professional researcher, one who searches databases on a daily basis, to help you narrow your search and quickly find the information you are looking for.

Business Data and Intelligence

The business of America is business, and judging by the copious quantity of data available on every aspect of it, that is as true today as ever. Through using the various available business databases, you can easily and quickly find officer profiles, business affiliations, pertinent financial information such as stock data, legal reviews and newspaper clips, sales figures, basic goals, employment information, locations and size of plants, production, distribution, industry trends and forecasts, marketing intelligence, technological developments, and sales.

Some major sources for such data are Prentice-Hall Legal and Financial Services, Dow Jones News/Retrieval, Mead Data Central, Dialog, Disclosure II, and Western Union InfoMaster. These sources have access to an amazing range of data, including databases such as Dun & Bradstreet, SEC filings, Moody's, and Standard and Poor's index, to name a few. (Dun & Bradstreet reports provide financial background, public record filing, and credit information about many businesses. Moody's and Standard and Poor's are business-related databases that provide financial information on-line from a variety of financial periodicals.) If you know how and where to look, there's almost no end to the amount of business information you can get on a company, its officers, and even its business intentions.

Putting It All Together

The information I have included in this chapter is just a beginning; it doesn't even scratch the surface of records and information available from all the on-line sources. There are so many database sources that I can't begin to describe them all or to keep up with the new ones coming on-line every day. To learn more, read one of the recent books on the subject of databases, as well as some of the magazines devoted to the subject. They can give you a much more comprehensive idea of what is available so you don't overlook what may be an essential source. They also tell you how to access the information easily.

Cautions

Some words of caution: Don't sign up with a vendor who wants to sell you software and a computer. Also don't rush to hook up with database vendors without first having focused on your needs and learned how to request the right data.

When I was first learning, I went into a system, searching for information on a Fortune 500 company. When the service finished printing out material on my initial request, which had cost about $75, it asked me if I wanted a family tree on the company, filled with information on stockholders, manufacturing sites, everything. I replied, "Sure." When the computer was finally finished, I had a huge stack of paper, 99 percent of which did not pertain to my case. Even worse, I had run up a bill of $1,625.

The ability to get information rapidly and in your office is great. But you have to know what you need, how to get it, and, most important, when to stop.

WHO'S WHO—IN WHAT

Ah, vanity, thy name is woman.

That famous line might more accurately have said, "Professionals are the truly vainglorious beings." That's fine by me, because that helps me run background checks. It will help you, too, if you use who's who directories for the various professions and occupations. I'm not immune either, so don't think I'm making a value judgment. You'll find me listed in *Who's Who in Security* and *Who's Who in the South and Southwest*.

The fact is, almost every industry has a published who's who. These directories get their information from professional associations and by soliciting individuals who want to be listed. Because vanity is such a big deal, the professionals fill out a form and buy the book, often paying a membership fee as well, in order to be listed in the directory.

The Value of These Directories

What can you get from a who's who? Most contain these basic information categories:

- Identifying information such as name, business address, telephone number, marital status, and number of children
- Education and employment histories—But beware: this information is all self-reported
- Other valuable information such as your subject's areas of specialization, awards received, and interests
- Frequently, a photograph

The most obvious use for who's who directories is for general background information and for developing identifying information.

Obtaining Directories

It isn't difficult to get hold of the books or to get information from them. You can find them in most public libraries.

I knew one innovative private investigator who developed an elaborate ruse to get who's who data directly from the source. This investigator, too lazy to develop his own background information on professionals, made up a slick who's who application form with the graphics package of his personal computer, then sent it to professionals to fill out and mail back so as to be listed in their professional directory. He had the form sent to a mail drop in another city, then had it forwarded back to himself. So, there you go—information straight from the source.

I don't know for sure, but he might even have collected fees from the subjects, too. That way he could acquire their bank account number from the check, which he promptly destroyed.

You don't have to go through such an elaborate scheme to get the information you need. I've made it a habit to collect all the who's who directories I can. If you want to stick to one or just a few industries, then buy the directories and subscribe to their periodic updates. If you need more or don't know how to get them, either call the various associations or go to your local library and see what it has; then find out how to order them.

If you think you are going to need to check out many different industries, I have two suggestions: First, you could subscribe to a computer on-line network such as Dialog or CompuServe, public information suppliers of over 500 databases that include Marquis Who's Who, Medline, Professional Employment databases, and various other professional and technical information sources.

Second, if you don't want to buy a computer to search, find someone who subscribes to the databases in your area and resells searches on a one-shot basis. As mentioned earlier, such services are information resellers or gateways—part of a new cottage industry in the making.

6

TRICKS OF THE TRADE

How do the best investigators produce time after time? How do they solve cases and find information that no one else can unearth? What magic do the real pros weave to find bank accounts, secret lovers, hidden assets, and undisclosed information that no one else can get?

Ask any good investigator about his or her secrets, about how he or she gets information without the use of a computer, the courthouse, or midnight trash runs. Before answering you, the investigator most likely will make sure no one else is within earshot, then whisper these secrets of success to you, if he or she is willing to talk at all. The best investigators will tell you that their time-tested "tricks of the trade" are pretexts, little white lies that are passed down like secret recipes, that produce when nothing else works.

PRETEXTS

Pretexts are a time-honored tradition in the investigative world and are passed down from one generation to another, from detective to street cop, from investigator to investigator. They're jealously hoarded like pearls in an oyster or diamonds in a vault.

The true secret of the supersleuths is often a glib-tongued, smooth-talking little pretext, a white lie that often falls into the gray area, but not illegal, realm of the law. By using pretexts, you can almost always get people to tell you what's in their heart and mind because they believe you can do something for them.

The true silver-tongued devil creates a story or scenario whereby the subject believes there is a possibility he or she will get something for free or, by helping our little devil, benefit in some way, either monetarily or by getting a job done without any hassle.

How do pretexts work? The best of them are perfectly logical, perfectly reasonable, and fit within the scope of our everyday lives. To be successful, you must let the story flow right out of your mouth, just as if it were true. Once you stutter and stammer, the effect is lost, and the credibility of the pretext disappears.

The secret of being able to use pretexts is practice, practice, practice. That, coupled with a developed mind-set that makes you believe you are in the role of the story you are using, makes the pretext plausible. You must be able to roll the pretext right off your tongue and improvise an answer to any question that your subject may throw at you.

What are the pretexts that work, and how are they applied? The following pretexts are used by investigators all over the country and have produced results when all else has failed.

Telephone Pretexts

The pretext that most people "in the business" use is the telephone pretext. It's quick, timely, cheap (in terms of effort and money expended), and invisible (if done right). No one sees you in person; you are only an anonymous voice over the wire.

Have you ever tried to find an old friend or lover and discovered his or her number has been disconnected? Or maybe you found a telephone number in your boyfriend's wallet, and when you dialed the number, the operator told you it had been disconnected and was no longer in service. Wouldn't you like to know who owned that number and where that person is now? This is where sweet talking comes in. The key is to believe (and make your telephone contact believe) that you are the party to whom they are speaking.

The Telephone Repair Pretext When you have only a phone number and need a name and address, dial the number in question, let it ring once, then hang up. Repeat this several times, then dial a third or fourth time and let the phone ring until someone answers.

When your party comes on the line, pound one of the buttons on your phone three or four times, sending a screeching signal through the phone. Then give it a loud "Hello, hello, is anyone there? This is Bob Johnson of the Aldine (or whatever district) Field Office of Telephone Repair. Hello, hello?"

Your subject, after being frustrated by a phone that has rung only once several times, by now is certain that something is wrong with the phone. He or she will be more than happy to talk to a telephone repairperson about the problem.

Explain that there has been a transformer burned out or a three-car collision with a pole down in the subject's district and that you are closing down this exchange and rerouting important lines to another transformer station while the company works on the problem. As a telephone repairperson, you are checking the few numbers left working in this exchange to determine if they are commercial businesses or homes in need of emergency service—those being homes with people having medical problems, young children, and the elderly—because they have a priority for repair work.

In many cases, your subject will say he or she needs to keep service up because of one of these emergencies (whether it is true or not) and ask that you keep his or her lines open and transfer them to another exchange so that service won't be out for a day or two. (It's amazing how many people don't want their phone lines disconnected for even this amount of time and will tell you any story and give you any information just to keep their service up.)

As a good repairperson, you say that you'll try to get the phone back in service within an hour but that you will need a little more information so you can see which of the already overloaded stations is nearest the subject's house and can take the calls for the next few days until normal service resumes. To do this, you say, "Give me a hundred block and street name so that I can find you on my service map."

The "customer," not having been asked for an exact street address, does not feel threatened and will give the street name and block number without batting an eye. You can either thank your subject and get off the line or visit for a few more minutes, asking, "Is that a house or an apartment complex?" If it's an apartment, then you need the name of the complex and the unit number, because there are so many phones in the complex that you won't be able to distinguish the subject's line.

Once you have gotten this basic information, tell the subject to check the phone again in fifteen or twenty minutes and to call telephone repair if service is not restored at that time. Then explain that you have to log in and verify the repair order, so you need a last name of the customer for the time log. (Explain that this is the phone company's security system to make sure repairpeople don't pull numbers out of the air when working overtime on emergencies.)

Your subject will be so happy that you kept up the phone service that your subject will have no problem giving you a name and often an exact home street address. If you don't get the street address, it is very easy to determine this information once you have the last name and street block. You can use on-line directory services, voter registration records, or a drive-by of the neighborhood to collect license plates. Ninety-five percent of the time, the whole job is done with this one phone call.

Sweet Talking Years ago, a canny investigator came up with a pretext to get the name and last address listed with the phone company for disconnected phone numbers. The pretext goes something like this.

Dial the phone company's business office for the telephone exchange (the first three numbers) and ask for the business operator for the particular exchange. Once you get the operator, explain that you are a marketing representative for a major national corporation and that the telephone number you want to know about has been identified by your company as one that meets the particular sequence of letters that you wish to use in a national media and advertising campaign. You have already determined by dialing the number that it is no longer in service, and you wish to reserve this number for your major corporation and obtain rights for your company to use it.

Once the operator verifies that the number is no longer in service, she will take your order and begin the paperwork to assign this number to your company. As the operator does this, explain that you have one other problem: to obtain a legal release from the last person who had the phone number.

Your company, you explain, requires not only a signed agreement with the phone company, but a release from the last owner of the phone number in order to preclude any legal problems or liability on the part of your company from any previous owners of that telephone number. You therefore need the name and last listed address or forwarding address of the last owner of the phone number so you can mail that person a release and a check for $500 to obtain consent to use the phone number.

Because you are buying this phone number and adding it to what evidently is a major account of the telephone company, and because you are bestowing upon some lucky person a $500 check for something that person has already given up, the operator will always give you the information you need.

If the address the operator has is no longer valid, you still have the name of the party who owned the phone number. You can check this name against all of the previously discussed public records sources and locate a date of birth or Social Security number from voter registration, marriage license, or other personal records, then proceed to find a new address through either a driver's license search, an employment examination, or new utility service.

The Deliveryperson

Many times, an investigator can locate the apartment complex a person lives in, but has difficulty determining the specific unit where the person is staying. I have found that the best way to determine which apartment your subject lives in is to begin by trying to call the complex or, if necessary, go there in person with flowers or a package, stating that you are attempting to deliver a present—preferably flowers, chocolates, or something perishable—to the individual from a loved one or friend.

Frequently, the apartment manager will give you the apartment number, especially if you telephone between 5:30 and 6:00 P.M., the time the apartment management office usually closes. Explain to the manager that your driver is now on the way to the office from his last stop and that the gift will not be deliverable the next day. Your excuse can be that the gift is perishable or that it is Friday and you don't deliver on weekends. As the supposed dispatcher, you need to persuade the apartment manager that the gift is real and that prompt delivery is crucial.

You can also use variations of this pretext. For example, you can claim you are delivering a money order so that a son or daughter can pay the rent (good near the first of the month), a travel agent delivering a ticket so a customer can fly home for the weekend or make a late-night business flight, or a hospital staff person giving the results of medical tests so that the resident can get married.

Announcing a Windfall

Everybody in the world hopes to inherit a fortune someday or dreams of being an heir to oil wells or some type of windfall. Some people even dream of winning the magazine sweepstakes and being "a winner for life." You can pretend to bring a little light into such a person's life by identifying him or her as a family member of a possible winner or heir and thereby determine the subject's date of birth, Social Security number, family tree, and former places of residence.

Just call up the person you are investigating, and announce that you're looking for a Floyd Riley (your subject's name) who is an heir to a claim dating back to 1925. (No one knows where the whole family was in 1925.)

Just paint a little picture of the inheritance. (The Riley family homesteaded property in Louisiana that was taken over by the Levee Control Board, and this land, which now has fifty oil wells on it, has been ordered by the state to be returned to its original owners.) The subject of your search will give you every family member he or she ever knew and any information you want that will help you identify him or her as a possible heir. You'll also brighten your subject's life for at least several weeks.

You wonderful person, you!

TRASH

Any good investigator will tell you that one of the best ways to find out what's going on in someone's house is to bag the household's trash. The debris of our lives goes in the garbage can and becomes fair game for the astute "garbageologist" who sifts through the envelopes, liquor bottles, handwritten notes, and doodles that we consign to the dump.

What You Can Learn

What do these bits of trash tell us? What secrets can be found amidst the eggshells and pizza crusts tossed out? Consider the following items, and think about what they reveal.

Envelopes Almost all letters, business or personal, have a return address on their envelope. That way, if the letter has insufficient postage or becomes undeliverable for any reason, it can be returned to the sender for remailing. These envelopes tell the garbage-smart investigator what bank the subject deals with. (Bank statements usually come at the end of the month and can be found in the weekend's trash.) People also toss out the envelopes from creditors, which pinpoint credit card carriers, department store accounts, medical service providers, psychiatrists, and dentists. If an investigator is lucky, those handwritten personal envelopes may list the return address of a subject's lover, intimate friend, or family member who sends notes on birthdays, holidays, and other special occasions.

119

Beer, Wine, and Liquor Bottles From the number of beer, wine, or liquor bottles, it is possible to establish a pattern and frequency of drinking, an issue often of interest to investigators involved in a domestic case. This evidence is particularly important with regard to the fitness of certain parents to care for their children. The existence of alcohol or drug dependency helps provide the attorneys in court with a picture of the opposing party's abuse problems and often documents perjury in personal testimony where the person claims to have none of these habits.

Personal Notes and Doodles Almost anyone who has ever planned a crime, fraud, or scheme of any kind has written it all out on paper, just to see what it looks like. In the hope of winning big profits or making big deals, people list the steps they have to take to get there, what they'll do with the money once they get it, and where they're going to go to live a life of luxury.

By intercepting this information through the trash, a good investigator can "read the mind" of the subject of investigation and show the client or a jury the planning of the opposing party or accused, straight from the source. Often investigators find detailed maps or diagrams of plans prepared by their subject, plans that outline the conspiring parties, their path in the plan, and other choice tidbits of condemning information.

Miscellaneous Items By sifting through the trash, you can find items that get thrown out of your subject's pockets, items that tell where your subject has been and what he or she has done. Matchbook covers disclose favorite watering holes, parking tickets disclose automobile locations. Receipts your subject wants to hide from his or her spouse are often tossed in the trash before they are ever brought into the house.

Thus, every piece of trash or garbage is a piece in the investigator's puzzle. It will fit into the overall scheme if you only know where to place it.

Getting the Trash

How can you get this trash? If it's put out on the curb the night before, you can simply drive by at 3:00 A.M., pop your trunk, and slide the garbage into the trunk of your car with no one the wiser.

But what if your subject doesn't make things easy for you? What if your subject keeps the trash well up in his or her yard, and the garbage collectors come up to the house, pick up the trash bags, and carry them back to the truck? What do you do then?

The simplest way to still get access to the trash is to offer a small inducement to the collectors of this precious information source. Once I have established the garbage pickup days and times, I meet the garbage truck driver at least a block before my subject's house. Then I establish a meaningful dialogue that includes a twenty-dollar bill. I make the driver familiar with the face of Andrew Jackson, fold the bill in half, and cut it through the middle. I then explain to the driver the address of the trash that I wish to collect. I hand over half the twenty-dollar bill and a good, strong Hefty trash bag, the kind that doesn't tear or fall apart when filled with the weekend's discards.

The driver soon understands that once the garbage is deposited in my bag and driven to the end of the next block, I'll be waiting with the other half of Andrew Jackson's likeness, and the driver's morning will be twenty dollars richer.

POTPOURRI

Be Creative . . . Never Give Up

All the records and sources I've mentioned so far, and my suggestions for using them, only scratch the surface of the many possibilities open to you in your investigations. So be creative and adapt to your situation.

Remember, to be able to search for information, you only need to know or suspect that it is available. Before you assume a record or information isn't public, ask for it or try to get it. Often, you'll find people and organizations cooperative when you didn't expect them to be and, indeed, when they didn't need to be. Even if you have doubts about getting the information, search for the best way to get it—through request, interview, subpoena by the police or your lawyer, or bugging your sources until they finally help you just to get you off their backs.

Pulling Rabbits from Hats

During my years as an investigator, I've collected every professional journal, city directory, phone book, reference guide, and voter registration census my shelves will hold. This readily available information coupled with persistence, has often enabled me to "pull rabbits out of hats." By combining these sources of identifying information with computer on-line data services, I've freed myself to search more esoteric sources and become able to draw conclusions from seemingly unrelated bits of information.

For example, I've gotten bowling records from the American Bowling Congress, addresses from hunting and fishing licenses, medical records from the Federal Aviation Administration, and found former Playboy Bunnies via Hugh Hefner's security chief. Once, my firm cracked a major voting fraud case by piecing together out-of-town utility bills, voter registrations, and probate records in order to prove that the dead had indeed risen from the grave to make their political choices known by voting in a local election.

Remember that no matter how well someone tries to hide out, that person almost always has blind spots. So much information is gathered on us in this country, and so much paper documentation is created, that it's next to impossible to hide out completely or totally cover your tracks. In one lifetime, a person's activities and involvements generate many more personal records and documents than most of us realize.

Charge Card Information If you creatively take advantage of these records, you, too, can pull some rabbits from hats. For example, you often can use charge cards as a source of information about people covering their tracks—errant husbands, check kiters trying to get their money out of the country, or slick con artists. In the case of an errant husband, he might forget and write his girlfriend's license plate number on gasoline charge receipts, or he might be out of cash and pay for a hotel room by charging the bill to his company. Charge card receipts and statements can give you up-to-date information on where your subject is eating, staying in hotels, traveling, or purchasing gas.

How can you find out who is the most important person in your subject's life? Try hotel phone charge records. Hotels keep a record of all long-distance telephone calls charged to a room. My experience is that after dinner and a few drinks, an errant spouse goes back to the hotel room and gets on the phone with that special someone closest to him. The first call is often to the one he wishes he were with, and that's not always the one he's married to. The *second* call is almost always to his wife.

Getting the Information Hotels and charge card companies will not always come across with the information you need just because you ask them to. But go ahead and ask anyway. You might get lucky.

If your needs are serious and involve a lawsuit, you might seek legal help by getting and using a subpoena to obtain these records from the hotel and charge card company. If you don't want to or can't do that, and you have gone as far as you can alone, you might hire a professional investigator to help get what you need. Often, professional investigators have developed working and trusting relationships or have traded out enough favors to get cooperation, so they can get information from difficult sources when others can't.

Remember, if you know that a record is likely to exist, if your purpose in checking out the information is important enough, and if you believe you need the documentation, then go after it. Chances are, you *will* need the documentation, especially if you have serious reasons for your search. Records provide more credibility than personal testimony.

A good example of why it is often better to use records to establish credibility and not personal testimony is a divorce case in which the client alleged that his wife had been having an affair with another man for several years while he (the client) was overseas on business. The wife admitted to knowing the alleged boyfriend but said she had met him only since her husband had filed for divorce, not before the couple had separated.

Our investigation of the client's gasoline credit card charges indicated that gasoline was charged to the co-respondent's automobile not only during the period of time when the husband was overseas but for more than three years before the separation as well. Guess who the jury believed?

Special Days and Holidays

Often, *when* a public record on your subject is made or the *time* your subject slips and shows his or her true self can be almost as important in searches as where to find the record. Certain days of the year are magic to any investigator. Through years of experience, investigators know that on these days, people will perform certain rituals or call home to family and loved ones. These are the days smart investigators focus on, to see people as they really are and where they are hiding from the rest of the world.

On these days, people show their soul and give us an insight into how they would really like to be or how they really are when no one is watching. To find out what we want to know, we need only focus on these magic days and document what transpires on them.

St. Valentine's Day The day for lovers is also the day to find someone's secret heartthrob. Look to see if your sub-

125

ject has bought any extra Valentine's Day cards or makes any long-distance phone calls. This is also a day to check for flower receipts on the Visa or American Express cards, as well as purchases of perfume or candy that did not go to your subject's home.

St. Patrick's Day If your subject doesn't come home on St. Patrick's Day, then he or she is probably out partying with some other young lassie or laddie. A subject who is wearing the green and comes home with a wee touch of the Irish may be kissing more than the Blarney stone.

Easter People tend to remember their mother on Easter Sunday, and they may call collect. That makes Easter an excellent day to find people by checking their mother's long-distance phone bill.

Mother's Day An even better day to find a missing someone who may call home to momma is Mother's Day. I would never advise anyone to read someone's mail, but the envelopes may be in the trash of the next garbage pickup. The postmark will tell what town the Mother's Day cards came from.

Memorial Day Almost all of us get out and do something on Memorial Day, whether we need to or not. If you really want to determine whether someone is physically capable of exercise or truly disabled from an injury, this is one of the best days to give that person your best eyeball.

Father's Day Not as many children call home to dad, but Father's Day is still a good day to check when looking for errant sons and daughters who can't be found in any other way.

Halloween The one night of the year that people show their true colors is definitely Halloween. If you have any doubt whatsoever about someone's sexual preference, this is the night when people strut their stuff, dressing up as their favorite fantasy and letting it all hang out. If you wonder whether or not someone bats both ways, this is the night to find out.

Thanksgiving Since Thanksgiving is a major day for family gatherings, it's a good time to find out how you rate with your beloved's family. If your intended won't take you home to momma now, there's a serious problem you'd better uncover before going any further in a relationship.

Christmas Another excellent time to check the credit card receipts is Christmas. Look for jewelry, perfume, and gift purchases that do not make it home. (Don't believe the lies that they went to someone else in the office.)

It's also a time to watch out for the little office parties and those special relationships that get fostered among all the good cheer. If a spouse is running late these days, there's a good chance he or she is not alone.

New Year's Eve If your subject leaves home for a few hours to take care of some last-minute errands or solve some little business problem, my hunch is that he or she is not alone. Check the mileage on the car, and divide it by two. This will give you the distance to whomever your subject is going out to see. Narrow down the area by seeing where the gasoline charges are, and you can pretty well pinpoint the location where the fun is taking place.

COLLECTING YOUR COURT JUDGMENT

The need for investigative work often arises even after someone has won a lawsuit. If you sue somebody (or represent a party to a lawsuit), it would be nice to think that once you have gone through the full legal process, won the case, and obtained a substantial judgment, all you have to do is reap the rewards. But do you?

What happens when you perfect your judgment, the prosecuted party or client refuses to pay his or her debt, and you find that the sheriff or constable cannot find enough assets to satisfy your judgment? What do you do next?

The first thing that comes to the mind of most attorneys is to depose the subject party in a postjudgment discovery action to determine that person's net worth and locate the source of his or her assets. Your lawyer makes the opposing party bring in financial statements, tax returns, and bank statements, and questions him or her about income and personal and business assets, in hopes of finding enough money to satisfy your judgment. But in conducting postjudgment discovery, many attorneys find that the opposing parties have already hidden their assets by taking the money offshore, transferring it to other entities, such as their children's or family trusts, or hiding it in another name. (Want a little secret on where to look? Try the spouse's maiden name. You will find the money there nine times out of ten.)

In twenty years of investigation, I have heard almost every story that can be dreamed up about how someone

128

has lost his or her assets and is no longer able to pay our judgment. These are some of the typical stories:

- I went to Las Vegas or Atlantic City and lost it all gambling.
- My wife and I used the money to live on and spent it all.
- My bookkeeper or accountant stole the money.
- I lost it all on bad business deals I entered trying to raise the money to pay this judgment.

Discovering "Hidden Assets"

If you hear these or similar stories and find that your opposition cannot document that the money disappeared as claimed, take advantage of these suggestions, which can point you to where the money has really gone. First, check the subject's home mortgage, and see if your subject paid down the mortgage during the period of the lawsuit by making several big payments, especially in the last year of your lawsuit. Many people try to hide their assets by paying down their mortgage and adding to the equity of their home, which, at least in Texas, they believe to be "bulletproof" because of the homestead law.

Examine the payments on your subject's universal life or whole life insurance policies. It's possible to make a prepayment that gathers interest just like a savings account but doesn't show up on financial records anywhere except inside the insurance policy itself.

Look for purchases of savings bonds in the subject's name, his or her children's name, or the wife's maiden name. Until recently, these transactions were not centrally registered and were a favorite purchase of money launderers and drug dealers.

Look for cashier's check purchases in your subject's bank accounts. These checks can be purchased and tucked away for the future just like cash.

When your lawyer brings the opposing party to a deposition, he or she can enhance the discovery process dramatically by making that person bring the kind of documents that will really help you or your investigator trace the person's financial history. This is one of the most overlooked areas of discovery, mainly because lawyers often don't understand the process of investigation. It is often more important to know where a person went and who that person spoke to or dealt with than to know where his or her business and money was months or years ago, when those last financial statements and tax returns were filed. Sometimes you can find the most crucial evidence by tracing the timing of certain activities, proving that financial transactions were made in preparation for protecting personal assets.

Key Documents

Certain key documents reveal a person's "inner mind" and help the attorney and investigator discover hidden assets and prove the intent of hiding these assets from the court. These documents include the following:

- *Passport*—The next time your lawyer subpoenas someone, have the motion for production ask that person to bring his or her passport. This document will prove, through the entry and exit visa stamps, the trips to Switzerland, the Cayman Islands, the Bahamas, the Isle of Man, and the Netherlands Antilles that you believe were made to hide money in foreign countries. (One accountant I know makes a trip to the Cayman Islands every month with his scuba gear. It took U.S. Customs three years to figure out his tanks were filled with $100 bills.) By documenting withdrawals from bank accounts and timing these with trips to foreign countries, we can often discover and document funds being transferred offshore.

- *Telephone records*—Many smart lawyers request business or personal phone records in the discovery process, but many don't think to include their subject's mobile or car phone records. It's good to remember that standard telephone records itemize only long-distance calls, but mobile phone records itemize all calls, local and long-distance, for billing purposes. If you want to find an undisclosed business partner (or a meaningful other in a relationship), try having your lawyer subpoena the car phone records and compare the names against the people that are known to your client. I promise that you will find some very interesting information.

- *Credit card statements*—As mentioned earlier in this book, these records document out-of-town travel and often name parties with whom your subject may have had dinner or done business, people who may well be pertinent to your investigation. These records also indicate what hotel your subject has stayed in, which gives you another interesting piece of information.

- *Hotel records*—Also mentioned previously, every hotel bill invoices not only for the room, meals, and drinks, but also for the long-distance telephone service used from the room. Calls from hotel rooms are often made to people we wouldn't call from home, such as an out-of-town banker, business associate, or lover.

- *Credit reporting agencies*—The trail of credit purchases follows us around the world. Like expense accounts, it lists where we eat, stay, and make purchases. It also contains a record of other business entities and banks that inquire about our financial status, once we have begun a financial relationship with them. Credit card inquiries are one of the best ways to locate undisclosed bank accounts, insurance policies, and other major purchases.

- *Airline travel*—When questioning a party about his or her business activities and assets, ask for the name of the person's travel agency. Once you have this information, your lawyer can send another subpoena to the travel agency to document all the trips, in every city, made by the subject of your investigation.

- *Telex*—When investigating a company's assets, consult the company's telex records to find foreign business entities, foreign bank accounts, and other offshore activities. The monthly telex log or bill will point you in the right direction.

- *Overnight packages*—Today almost every business and many individuals use overnight couriers such as Federal Express to deliver valuable mail and packages around the world. An examination of the monthly bills of a company's overnight packages gives a good, clear idea of what cities and countries the company is doing business in.

132

All of the records listed are easily obtained if your lawyer requests them under a motion for production. If you find that the opposing party is unwilling or unable to produce these documents (another one of the great stories is that all of those records were destroyed), that should raise a red flag and make you consider urging your lawyer to subpoena these records directly from their sources.

In many cases, once these records were requested, obstinate parties have suddenly become much more amenable to resolving financial issues and settling their judgments. If they have anything to hide, they would much rather settle with someone who appears experienced in such matters than have these records made public for other creditors to find as well.

The next time you and your lawyer go into postjudgment discovery (or if you want to find the financial worth and assets of parties earlier on in a case), consider these ideas and resources for your legal strategy.

MANHUNTS, DETECTIVE-STYLE

Maybe someone is missing from your life—a former lover, a lost friend to whom you owe a debt, or a family member who has disappeared from the Christmas card list. With the advent of computers and the increasing availability of databases on every sport, profession, and industry, tracking people has become much easier for the entrepreneurial detective or at-home investigator. You just have to know enough about the people you're searching for—their hobbies, the work they do, the state or region of the country where they last lived—and you can develop information to profile them and obtain their date of birth, Social Security number, and enough other vital information to track them down, not only in this country, but worldwide.

Looking for Love

If I've learned anything at all from the thousands of investigations my firm has conducted for people looking for love, it can be summed up in this one line: If someone sounds too good to be true, he or she probably is.

The reason most people come to me in the first place is that somewhere in their being a warning bell has gone off. Their mind tells them something their heart doesn't want to listen to and whispers to them in the dark that all is not as it seems.

Considering all the cases in which I've checked out personal relationships, I'd say almost 70 percent of the people I investigated hid something, minor or major, from their potential mate. Some of these cases contain little white lies—exaggerated educations or backgrounds, or puffed up descriptions of personal achievements and accomplishments. These small things I consider normal, and I tell my clients this is to be expected. We all see ourselves through rose-tinted glasses, and our personal admissions are more often of our ambitions, not our actual accomplishments.

However, every so often, I run across people who can really hurt you, the ones you need to watch out for—the sociopaths and pathological liars who prey on the single set. How bad can they hurt you? Let's take a look and see:

Carolyn, with several of her friends, liked to spend weekend nights at Studebakers, a Houston upscale singles bar. She went to dance, drink, and search for a mate. Late one Saturday night, Carolyn met Trent, liked his dark curly hair and winning smile, and took him home.

Over the next three weeks, Trent told her everything she wanted to hear: He had been orphaned at an early age and had never found love. Through the terrible fire that had killed his parents, he had inherited a business and a large trust fund that had put him through college and would support him for life. He was now established as a successful engineer with a solid future.

After being together just a month, the couple planned a gorgeous riverboat wedding. Carolyn rang up seven thousand dollars in charges for the wedding, assured by Trent that he'd pay for all expenses out of his trust account.

Carolyn's first warning should have been that Trent had no proof of identification when they went to the county clerk's office to apply for their marriage license. Carolyn had brought her birth certificate and driver's license, but Trent just couldn't seem to find his, and he said, "Let's take the papers home, and I'll fill them out and mail them in after the ceremony."

Three weeks later, when the marriage license still hadn't come back, Carolyn became suspicious. She questioned Trent's stories and activities, then came to me after she found that the car she had thought was his was instead registered to another woman.

A quick search of courthouse records revealed more than Carolyn ever wanted to know. Trent was fifty-one years old, not the thirty-six he had claimed. He had been married at least three times before. A warrant for his arrest had been outstanding for the past two years. Court records indicated he had abandoned a wife and two children, had never paid a cent of child support to his former family, and had lived with women all over the state, using four different variations of his real name. And what of the woman who owned the license plates to his car? Well, she had lived with Trent for the last eight months, on and off, and she was quite happy to have him still visit once or twice a week, even though she knew he'd just been married.

If only the truth about Trent had ended there. But the worst was yet to come. One of Trent's ex-wives told me that he had given her a nasty social disease—the kind that doesn't go away. Trent had never graduated from college, and there was no inheritance or trust fund. And even worse yet, a co-worker told me that Trent was a psychopath who was under investigation for the disappearance and death of two young girls in Mexico.

Listening to the truth about Trent, Carolyn came apart before my eyes. She cried and then broke out in a scream of wrenching heartache and burning anger. Then she called Trent at the other woman's house. (Trent was supposedly in Atlanta for the weekend on a consulting job.) Very coldly, Carolyn told him that she knew about it all—his lies, his wives, and all the other terrible things he had done.

Trent didn't skip a beat. He told her that it simply wasn't true, that he could prove to her that all she had been told were lies, and that she should meet him at the airport so they could go away for the weekend and work it all out. "Just meet me at the Aero Mexico counter, baby, and I'll take care of everything," Trent assured her.

She went to the airport, but she wasn't alone. Two undercover police officers followed Carolyn to the ticket counter, just waiting to get their hands on Trent for the two-year-old arrest warrant. Trent didn't show, and he had made no reservations, so Carolyn walked through the terminal back toward her car in the airport parking lot, the police officers trailing a hundred feet behind.

As she emerged from the terminal, Trent's car sped by, swerved in front of her, screeched to a stop, and cut her off from the street. A pair of long, strong arms reached out through the open window, grabbed her, and pulled her toward the car.

With just seconds to spare, the police rescued Carolyn. They yanked Trent out of the car and made him spread-eagle on the trunk.

What would have happened if the police hadn't been there? Ask Carolyn if you ever see her. She'll tell you she's very happy to be alive.

Women aren't the only ones that fall into star-crossed situations. Some of the smartest businessmen I know are wide open to someone who stares longingly into their eyes and listens to them for a change.

For example, Bill Fogle was a successful businessman who had just gone through a midlife crisis. He divorced his wife of fifteen years, broke up a business partnership with his longtime friend, and began an intensive exercise program to build himself back up to where he could feel like he was twenty again. In this state of mind, Bill was ripe for picking.

With no one to come home to or share his daily problems, Bill began touring the local bars, eating out, staying late for drinks, and watching the other singles hustle each other until the wee hours of the morning. One of those nights, a young girl fresh into Houston ran headlong into Bill.

Bill was an ideal target. She could see the gold Rolex on his wrist, the sapphire pinky ring, and black BMW, all of which told Cindy that here was a man worth her time. He had the eyes of a droopy basset hound, and a look that said, "Take me away from all this," was written all over his face.

Cindy went home with Bill that night and didn't leave. Within two weeks, she was sizing up his office, telling Bill that she could manage it for him, and looking at a Mercedes convertible for herself. Cindy told Bill how to dress and whom to see, and she began to bring in a friend of hers, a consultant she said could really help in his business.

Well, Bill was blind, but his employees weren't. They pegged Cindy as a gold digger right away. Bill's secretary gathered up Cindy's date of birth and Social Security number from the personnel file that she had just started, found Cindy's old address from her driver's license, and made an appointment with me to build a dossier on Cindy. (How did I meet Bill? We had been friends for years, and one day when I walked into his office to trade some property, I was stunned by his receptionist. I guess I still am because we got married in six weeks, and the honeymoon isn't over yet.)

With Cindy's Social Security number and date of birth, we found that she was from North Carolina and had left a trail of hot checks and petty theft charges, as well as two messy divorces that she had conveniently forgotten to tell Bill about.

The following week the company's secretaries took Bill out for lunch. I met them and laid out Cindy's past for Bill, as well as a little juicy information on her "consultant" friend, who was no stranger to white-collar crime.

Bill wouldn't believe it. He didn't want to believe it. He went home and told Cindy, who said it was all a pack of lies, after which he called me and asked if I could make this old information disappear. I told him he was nuts, that Cindy had all the earmarks of trouble, and that she would beat him out of his home and business within a year.

Three weeks later, Bill and Cindy got married, half of his company's employees were either fired by the consultant or pushed into quitting, and Cindy became the president of Bill's company. She got her Mercedes convertible, a three-carat diamond, and enough clothes from Neiman Marcus to fill Imelda Marcos's closet. Bill changed his will in Cindy's favor, cutting out his former wife and sons, and he took out a hefty life insurance policy at Cindy's suggestion of "just in case." Then he sank into a purple fog while Cindy began to clean him out.

Six weeks after their marriage, the honeymoon began to pall. Bill's friends, who had refused to come to the wedding, wouldn't talk to him. His creditors and suppliers were cutting off his company because their bills hadn't been paid. Finally, Cindy began to show her true colors. As soon as Bill began to turn down the money spigot, Cindy raged and screamed, throwing a telephone through a glass door, dishes across the house, and a knife in Bill's direction when he tried to get her to make love. All of a sudden, the fog before Bill's eyes began to lift, and he saw not an angel, but a barracuda, with glistening teeth.

The next year was truly a nightmare for Bill. His new wife had him in court like a revolving door, eating up his time and money for lawyer fees and the temporary support payments Cindy claimed she needed because she couldn't get a job due to her terrible emotional distress. Wherever Bill went, Cindy was right behind him, stalking him like prey. She threw things at him in restaurants, screamed at his friends in public, and even used a pair of scissors to stab the police officer who came to serve her with a restraining order to keep her away from Bill (just like in the movie *Play Misty for Me*).

Now, even though the divorce is done, Bill fears for his life because Cindy just won't go away. She stays the court-ordered seventy-five feet away from him but follows him through grocery stores, shopping malls, and baseball games just to haunt him, such is her obsession with him.

How would you like to be stuck with someone like this? Bill still is. If you don't think this happens in real life, just ask a few of your friends. I'll bet that at least one of them has had a situation like the last two I have just outlined for you.

Sports Fans

What is your subject's favorite sport? Whatever it is, I'll bet it's licensed and regulated, and your subject may subscribe to the special-interest magazine that's considered the bible of that sport. That publication's records will give your subject away every time. Also, every sport has its fan association and its official participation or sanctioning organization. These groups are wide open to your investigative skills. Just ask them, but don't tell why you are asking, and they will usually be all too glad to help.

Wherever someone runs to, wherever that person quietly slips away to, the last thing he or she will give up is a hobby or special interest, those little things that make life fun and worthwhile. Let's look at a few of them and see where they lead you.

Hunting and Fishing Licenses Almost every state in the country licenses residents and nonresidents who fish and hunt in the state. License fees are a source of revenue for replenishing and policing natural resources. Information about hunting and fishing licenses is in a state database, often at the state department of natural resources, a fish and wildlife department, or the department of revenue. Like most state records, these documents are open to anyone who asks to see them.

The files will reveal the name, address, date of birth, and often the Social Security number of anyone applying for a hunting or fishing license. Most important, the address must be current for out-of-state license applications, because the license is, in most cases, mailed back. Also, licenses are usually verified by another document such as a driver's license.

The following story illustrates just how crucial it can be to know your subject's special interests.

Steve, an avid hunter from Spokane, Washington, went out one night for a pack of cigarettes and never returned home. His wife and children, fearing foul play, called the police. They conducted a search for several days, then decided Steve had run off with another woman.

A year later, our investigators looked at the case and saw Steve had not renewed his Washington hunting license, but a license had been issued in Montana under the same name. We redirected our search and found him running a sporting goods store in a small hunting community. Steve couldn't believe we had tracked him to the tiny community, and to this day he doesn't know it was his passion for hunting that gave him away.

Motor Vessel Licensing Boat people—the ones you see living at marinas on sailboats, houseboats, and luxury yachts—have the option of pulling up anchor in the middle of the night and floating out with the tide. Some of them leave their debts and problems behind. They can be very hard to find unless you know to look up U.S. Coast Guard records and the records of the state boating registrar. Boaters may have to register only once a year, but often that's the only way you have to find these people.

Bowlers The American Bowling Congress (ABC) helped me find old friends I've lost track of over the years. Call them in Paramus, New Jersey, and ask what happened to that old bowling partner who was in your league. They'll tell you in which town his league record is being kept. They've got all the stats right there in their bowler database.

One of my most complex injury claims cases was settled when a man named Fred showed up in court for trial in a wheelchair, telling the jury how he'd suffered for four years with terrible back problems and a stiff neck, and was unable to raise his arm above his shoulder. There wasn't a dry eye in the jury box after this man described the physical discomfort he'd gone through, and his lawyer was anticipating a rewarding verdict.

Unfortunately for Fred, our first witness was someone from the American Bowling Congress we had subpoenaed to provide the past three years' league bowling records for this poor crippled man. The records verified that Fred's average had actually improved during the past three years and even listed the names of teammates who had bowled with him, as well as opponents. We had subpoenaed those people, and they were waiting to testify that Fred had not appeared crippled to them while he drank beer and managed a 187 average, pocketing the league's Most Improved Bowler cup.

Fred thought that because he had moved four times in a year under another name, he was invisible and could hide from the insurance investigators and lawyers trying to prove his injury was a scam. He had hoped to retire on workers' compensation but now faces perjury charges as a result of his testimony in court.

Football, Basketball, Baseball Fans of football, basketball, and baseball are heavily courted by advertisers, ticket sellers, colleges, and special-interest magazines. They buy season tickets months or years in advance, and they order their favorite team jackets, headgear, and pennants to demonstrate their support. By knowing someone's college and checking either their alumni association or athletic department, you can find out exactly where they're going to be on that special game day, most likely even in what seat. I once served court papers to a Saudi high roller who had walked out on an $850,000 debt he owed to a Las Vegas casino, and I did it just this way.

Remember all that advertising *Sports Illustrated* did to get people to collect goofy videos for subscribing to the magazine? Just imagine how big a database of sports fans *SI* must have and how much that could help you! *Sports Illustrated*, like many other magazines, sells its database of subscribers to businesses looking for sales leads. (As you probably know, that's why you get all that junk mail after you order a magazine subscription.)

When I was a federal agent, I learned the trick of

collecting subscription lists from my boss, who was tracking down a gang of jewel thieves. This sage detective obtained the mailing list of the fancy home and jewelry magazines and checked the subscription list for the names of known jewel thieves he was investigating. He found a whole gang by matching the subscription names against his FBI computer for arrests. The infamous Murph the Surf and his gang never did figure out that we nailed them by finding their address on a jewelry magazine subscription list.

Racing If your subject likes speed—whether it's sports cars, hot rods, powerboats, or motorcycles—he or she is likely to belong to a national organization in order to get a rating in that sport. Almost all racing associations now have safety requirements that include registration of members. They list where members race, include them in point standings for comparison against other racers, and have databases that follow them all over the country. If your guy or gal is on the racing circuit, you may even be able to predict where he or she is going to be next—and without a crystal ball.

CALLING IN A PROFESSIONAL

If you've exhausted all the tricks I've tried to teach you in this book but still haven't solved your problem, it's time to consider professional help. If you don't know a private investigator personally, let me suggest a few good ways of finding a reliable firm before you let your fingers take that stroll through the yellow pages. (It's been my experience that the ability of an investigative firm is inversely proportional to the size of its ad in the phone book.)

Like any professional you want to check out, such as an attorney or a doctor (and you do check out those folks—or you do now, anyway—right?), reliable investigators belong to professional associations. Many of the members are true experts in their field, and you can get a referral to them quickly by approaching the association.

The following list includes some of the most important investigator organizations and their phone numbers:

- *American Society for Industrial Security (ASIS)*, Arlington, Virginia (703-522-5800)—Security consultants, investigators, and industry professionals. ASIS is the largest association of security professionals. Its members are drawn from the investigative industry, police agencies on all levels, and private firms worldwide.

- *The Resource Line, ION, Inc.*, Tempe, Arizona (800-338-3463)—Referral and screening service that helps clients find the right investigator for them.

- *National Association of Certified Fraud Examiners*, Austin, Texas (800-872-4678)—Private investigators, auditors, accountants, and others interested in financial cases, internal audits, and money trouble. Members from industry, consulting, and investigative firms.

- *National Association of Investigative Specialists*, Austin, Texas (512-832-0355)—Private investigators and others interested in investigation. Also publishes numerous skills manuals on the investigative industry.

- *National Association of Legal Investigators*, Des Moines, Iowa (515-255-0569)—Members specialize in personal injury and other lawyer-oriented investigations; usually staff investigators for law firms and private investigators who work primarily in the legal profession.

- *World Association of Detectives*, Severna Park, Maryland (301-544-0119)—Private investigators (generalists and specialists) with diverse backgrounds, services, and clientele.

Many of the larger states also have their own private investigator groups. You can locate them through state licensing boards in the state capital or through referrals from local investigators.

How to Hire a Private Investigator

When I first joined this industry in the early seventies, there were few standards and just as few licensing rules. Almost anyone could set up shop, hang out a shingle, and offer services as a "private investigator."

After a lot of hard work, the industry has improved dramatically, policing and educating itself so that today private investigators are becoming true professionals. Many current operatives have college degrees in criminology, sociology, or accounting. They can seek certification through their trade associations to improve their skills and to gain mutual recognition from their peers.

Progressive states, such as California and Texas, require several years' experience in the field and a passing grade on a written test that demonstrates knowledge of the law and the industry. They also demand client protection through insurance bonds that pay any upheld claims levied against investigators or their agencies.

These state boards are excellent sources for determining the credibility of a private investigator and uncovering whether or not former clients or other parties have filed any complaints, charges, or grievances against that investigator. The licensing agencies also keep on file the backgrounds of individual investigators, and the information contained in their licensing applications is available to the public. These state bureaus can tell you how long a firm (or investigator) has been in business, how many offices and employees work for it, and the status of its license.

Besides contacting your state's licensing agency, check several references supplied by the investigator before you take out your checkbook to contract for services. (If the investigator you're considering hiring refuses to give you references, claiming client confidentiality or some other excuse, I suggest you take your business to a more professional firm.) The best references an investigator can suggest are lawyers, bankers, and other business clients, because they frequently have had more than one experience with the investigator.

From time to time, I have been asked as an expert witness to testify against other investigators who had overcharged clients, obtained information improperly or illegally, caused their client to be sued, or gotten into some other conflict with the client. Many of these cases would never have reached the lawsuit stage if the client had been able to use the information in this book to evaluate the investigator.

Before you hire someone to do your security or investigation, make sure that the person you're trusting your secrets to is legitimate. I promise that you will not want to hire somebody like the star of this little horror story:

Mickey Goodwin is the kind of investigator who will

promise you anything, tell you what you most want to hear, and then grab your money and run. The clients who hired him usually came to him as a last resort, often through dubious referrals, hoping Mickey could come up with the evidence to break a big case so they could get custody in a divorce or help plant evidence that would force their opponent into a conflict to settle a case.

To confirm that Mickey is his own worst client, all you have to do is check the cases on file in the local federal courthouse, captioned *United States v. Goodwin*. Our "hero" has been charged with altering court documents, theft, drug possession, and solicitation for prostitution. Check a little further, and you'll discover "Goodwin" isn't even his real name, but one he dreamed up because he had charges against the original in another state.

Mickey's former clients will tell you he took their thousand-dollar retainers and became invisible. His promises were as empty as his credentials were fake. Often, they discovered they were in worse trouble after hiring Mickey than they had been before, because they found themselves involved in legal actions his shenanigans had caused.

There's a special place in my "mean file" for the Mickeys of our business, because most of us in the investigative field have worked hard to build something we can all be proud of. With some help from educated clients, maybe we can get the Mickeys out of the trade and keep them out.

Now that you know what you can do to discover the truth about someone, remember: never hire any investigator to help you with a problem until you check out that person, too.

A FINAL WORD

The information and examples in this book are only the beginning rather than the end of this story. Our search for information is never-ending, with new chapters being written every day as con artists use their vast resources of intelligence and guile to stay ahead of the game, creating new schemes to separate honest people from their money.

Take what you've learned here and explore new territory. Develop your own means of ferreting out the truth. Remember, creativity is the key.

If you ever have a problem that you can't solve (after reading this book), leave it alone for a few days, then try to come back with a fresh approach. Sometimes your brain gets stale if you look at something too long or too hard. If that doesn't work and you feel it's worthwhile, give me a call at my office in Houston, Texas (713-880-1111), and I'll see if I can help.

Good luck and good hunting.

BIBLIOGRAPHY

Buckwalter, Art. *Investigative Methods*. Woburn, MA: Butterworth Publishers, 1984.

Fallis, Greg, and Ruth Greenberg. *Be Your Own Detective*. New York: M. Evans and Company, 1989.

Faron, Fay. *Take the Money and Strut!* San Francisco: Creighton-Morgan Publishing Group, 1988.

Ferraro, Eugene. *You Can Find Anyone*. Santa Ana, CA: Marathon Press, 1986.

Glossbrenner, Alfred. *How to Look It Up Online*. New York: St. Martin's Press, 1987.

Greene, Marilyn, and Gary Provost. *Finder*. New York: Crown Publishers, 1988.

Internal Revenue Service. *IRS Manual* (special agent handbook). Washington: U.S. Government Printing Office.

Investigative Reporters and Editors, Inc. *The Reporter's Handbook: An Investigator's Guide to Documents and Techniques*. New York: St. Martin's Press, 1983.

Kizorek, Bill. *Claims Detective*. Naperville, IL: PSI Publishing, 1987.

Kramer, W. Michael. *Investigative Techniques in Complex Financial Crimes*. Vienna, VA: National Institute on Economic Crime, 1991.

Lesko, Matthew. *Information U.S.A.* New York: Viking-Penguin, 1986.

Nossen, Richard A. *The Detection, Investigation, and Prosecution of Financial Crimes.* Richmond, VA: Richard A. Nossen and Assoc., 1982.

——. *The Seventh Basic Investigative Technique.* Richmond, VA: Richard A. Nossen and Assoc., 1975.

Noyes, Dan. *Raising Hell: A Citizen's Guide to the Fine Art of Investigation.* San Francisco: Mother Jones, 1987.

Pileggi, Nicholas. *Blye, Private Eye.* New York: Pocket Books, 1987.

Royal, Robert, and Steven Schutt. *The Gentle Art of Interviewing and Interrogation.* Englewood Cliffs, NJ: Prentice-Hall, 1976.

Slade, E. Roy. *Sweet Talking: The Pretext Book.* Austin, TX: Thomas Publications, 1991.

Smith, Edward. *Practical Guide for Private Investigators.* Boulder, CO.: Paladin Press, 1982.

Thomas, Ralph. *How to Find Anyone Anywhere.* Austin, TX: Thomas Publications, 1986.

Thomas, Ralph, and Edmund Pankau. *Investigator's Data Base and Records Research Training Manual.* Austin, TX: Thomas Publications, 1988.

U.S. Department of the Treasury. *Federal Law Enforcement Training Center, Criminal Investigator Training Division: Sources of Information.* Washington: U.S. Government Printing Office.

Williams, David C. *Investigator's Guide to Sources of Information.* Washington: U.S. General Accounting Office, 1988.

ABOUT THE AUTHOR

Edmund J. Pankau is the founder and president of Intertect, Inc., a Houston-based national private investigation agency. He has more than twenty years of investigative experience, both as a special agent in the U.S. Treasury Intelligence Division and as a private investigator specializing in corporate, legal, and financial investigations.

An accomplished speaker, Mr. Pankau conducts seminars throughout the United States on fraud examination, hidden asset location, and the new technology of the private investigator. He has authored numerous articles and has been featured in such publications as the *Wall Street Journal*, *USA Today*, the *New York Times*, *Time*, *Playboy*, and *Entrepreneur*. Some of his most famous investigations have been featured on "20/20," CNN's "Moneyline," "America's Most Wanted," "Inside Edition," "Donahue," "Geraldo," "Larry King Live!," and "Joan Rivers."

Mr. Pankau is the first investigator in America to hold all three professional certifications in his industry: CLI (Certified Legal Investigator), CFE (Certified Fraud Examiner), and CPP (Certified Protection Professional). He also has served on the advisory board of the Investigators Online Network, is a member of the American Society for Industrial Security insurance fraud committee, and serves on the board of regents of the National Association of Certified Fraud Examiners.

As a nationally recognized authority on investigator standards and technology, Mr. Pankau frequently consults as an expert in the field of financial fraud investigation and investigator industry standards.